A COGNITIVE APPROACH TO THE ETHICS OF COUNSELING PSYCHOLOGY

John William Dienhart
St. Cloud State University

UNIVERSITY
PRESS OF
AMERICA

LANHAM • NEW YORK • LONDON

University Press of America,® Inc.

4720 Boston Way
Lanham, MD 20706

3 Henrietta Street
London WC2E 8LU England

Library of Congress Cataloging in Publication Data

Dienhart, John William.
   A cognitive approach to the ethics of counseling
psychology.

   Bibliography: p.
   1. Moral development. 2. Values. 3. Counseling—
Moral and ethical aspects. 4. Kohlberg, Lawrence,
1927-   . I. Title.
BF778.D53   1983   174'.915   82-17393
ISBN 0-8191-2817-1
ISBN 0-8191-2818-X (pbk.)

For Colin

ACKNOWLEDGMENT

I would like to thank Hugh Chandler who helped me formulate the topic and guided me in the early going. James Wallace contributed in many ways. His comments and criticisms helped me with everything from clarifying small points to organizing the dissertation. William Alston made contributions to Chapter 1 which had ramifications for the entire work.

I am also very grateful to William Alston, Irene Lamkin and the Department of Philosophy at the University of Illinois for granting me office space during the academic year 1978-1979. This made the task of writing this much easier than it would have been otherwise. Ann Shaw was the final typist, and helped me with a great many technical points. Michael Morgan helped make stylistic revisions and also came to my rescue during the final proofreading.

The University of Toronto Press and Lawrence Kohlberg were also very helpful. They quickly and graciously gave me permission to quote liberally from the article, "Stages of Moral Development as a Basis for Moral Education," an article by Professor Kohlberg which appeared in Moral Education: Interdisciplinary Approaches (© University of Toronto Press, 1971).

I would also like to thank Terri and my son Colin who helped me through the difficult times that arise in the course of writing a work such as this.

Finally, my love and thanks go to my family, who gave me the courage to keep working when the task seemed futile. My mother deserves special thanks. She put up with a lot when I was in my youth and although she lived to see me educated, she did not live to see this book. I will miss her always.

TABLE OF CONTENTS

PREFACE

In 1977 I became involved with a self-help therapy group called Integrity Groups. It was founded by O. H. Mowrer who believed that the best way for people to deal with their problems was to talk openly and honestly to others who faced roughly similar problems. One thing that I noticed was that there was a great deal of specific advice offered on all sorts of issues concerning moral and non-moral values. However, there did not seem to be a problem with members blindly adopting the suggestions given to them. Sometimes people would agree to try to follow a suggestion to see if it worked, and often there was a great deal of discussion about the moral nature and practicality of suggestions. I began to realize that what we were doing was simply exchanging attitudes and thoughts about issues just as any group of people might do. The group was artificially constructed, but what we did in it was not.

As a student of ethics, I naturally became curious about what was going on. It appeared that the moral opinions of people ranged from simple egoism to sophisticated notions of justice and duty. It was around this time that I first encountered developmental theories of moral acquisition, which seemed to explain nicely both the dynamics of the group discussion and the wide range of moral values that were discussed. It occurred to me that it might be fruitful to analyze traditional psychoanalysis and therapy in general in light of the developmental model. My hope at that time was that such an analysis would contribute to redescribing the recurring problem of clients acquiring values in therapy as well as suggesting new ways to handle that problem. This book is an attempt to achieve those goals by examining such issues as the nature of morality, moral learning, and the problem of indoctrination. My thesis is that we cannot fully understand or properly evaluate the problem of clients acquiring values in therapy without understanding how these three issues fit together. Insofar as I am successful, a great deal of the credit should go to O. H. Mowrer and John Nicholls who took an interest in my work and helped me learn enough about psychology to complete it. I am, of course, solely responsible for any shortcomings.

CHAPTER 1

MORAL AND NON-MORAL VALUES IN THERAPY

1.0 Introduction

The advent of psychoanalysis initiated a
growing concern about the effects of therapy on
client beliefs. Moral and non-moral beliefs
describing a way of life (that is, a system of
values) are of special interest because one of the
things that goes on in therapy, from strict
analysis to informal counseling, is an alteration
of client beliefs. The question is, what role
should therapy play in this alteration? Should a
therapist actively reconstruct the values of a
client? Should the client be left alone in his
decisions about value? Should some "middle"
ground be sought? I will attempt to answer these
questions from a therapeutic and moral point of
view. I will show that there are therapeutic
reasons for allowing a client to develop his
values independently of therapy. There is also
the moral problem of violating a client's rights
by directly shaping his values. Although there
is a general (although not universal) agreement
that these are good reasons for a therapist to
leave the client's values alone, there is dis-
agreement about the possibility of achieving
this goal. I will argue that previous discussions
of this topic are unsatisfactory because they
fail to characterize adequately the influence
therapy has on a client's values. For example,
there is good reason to think that a therapist
should exert some influence on a client, otherwise
there would be no point to therapy. But what is
the nature of this influence, and how is it
related to influencing values? How do we discriminate between acceptable and unacceptable influence?
Many attempts to answer this question have been
hampered by their avoidance of two central issues:
what a value system is, and how persons acquire

1

and maintain value systems. If we do not have a fairly good idea of what it is to have a moral system, how can we know if therapy affects it? Further, if we do not know how people acquire and maintain value systems, we cannot estimate the impact of therapy on client values.

In this dissertation I will try to show that moral beliefs and beliefs about the good life cannot be eliminated from therapy. The kind of problem this presents for therapy will depend on the conception of morality and moral learning on which one relies. If morality and moral acquisition are essentially non-rational, then it will be virtually impossible to prevent a client from adopting therapeutic values. If, however (as I will argue), morality and moral development have significant rational components, we can prevent non-rational adoption of values in therapy by urging the client to examine those values critically.

I will not address questions such as the client's right to confidentiality. I do not deny that this is an important question, it is simply one I will not discuss. The problem of confidentiality arises only in special circumstances: the client threatens to kill himself or to destroy large amounts of property. If a therapist has such information, there are good reasons both to tell the proper authorities and to keep the information a secret. The integrity of the therapeutic relationship is in conflict with general moral duties. The question with which I am concerned arises even when therapy is free of such specific problems. As we shall see, it concerns the nature of therapy itself.

In this first chapter I will present and critically examine the value-free thesis, which was the first attempt to understand and cope with the effect of therapy on clients' moral and important non-moral beliefs. In order to clarify the value-free thesis, I will briefly examine how

the term 'value' is used in the context of
therapy. This will prepare us for 1.2, where I
explain the value-free thesis. In sections 1.3-
1.3.2 I will point out some difficulties with
this thesis. Finally, in 1.4, I admit that
these difficulties constitute serious objections
to the value-free thesis, but that this does not
warrant rejecting all aspects of the value-free
thesis.

1.1 Two Uses of 'Value'

The term 'value' has many uses. As Frankena
points out, values and value problems can range
over "the good, the end, the right, obligation,
virtue, aesthetic judgment, the beautiful, truth
and validity."[1] Luckily, we do not need to sort
out the relations among these various uses. When
I talk about the problem of values in therapy I
am not talking about the aesthetics of the practice
of therapy or whether this practice might be
obligatory or right, although these questions can
be asked. The problem on which I will concentrate
is the effect of therapy on <u>beliefs</u> clients have
about some of these values, viz., moral and non-
moral values which help to determine a way of
life. How does therapy affect a client's view of
what is morally obligatory, or morally right? How
does it affect non-moral issues, such as a choice
of career, or whom to marry? Therapy can affect
these beliefs in two ways. It can help alter:

    a)   Principles which form the basis of
          evaluative judgments.
    b)   Particular evaluative judgments.

Normally, we expect that a change in one of
these areas results in or indicates a change in
the other. If a person becomes a religious
convert adopting the creed of a particular religion,
we would expect that some of his particular judgments would change. Similarly, if a person's
particular judgments change, this is often a good
reason to think that more basic beliefs have

3

changed.

Although a and b are related in the way just
described, it must be recognized that a change in
one does not necessitate a change in the other.
A person could change his principles without
changing particular judgments if the new principles
supported those previous judgments. Further, a
person could change previous judgments without
changing principles if he discovered that he was
not applying those principles correctly. Therapy,
then, can affect both what we judge to be important, and why we make those judgments. Which
aspect of a client's values is more important is
something we will have to examine. It will become
apparent that lack of attention to the distinction
between a and b has been one source of confusion
in discussions on this problem.

In what follows I will use the word 'value' to
indicate the moral and non-moral values determining
a way of life, whether these values concern
a) basic principles or b) particular judgments.
It is necessary to lump a and b together in this
chapter since very few writers observe the distinction. The differences between a and b, and
its relevance to our problem, will become evident
in Chapters 2 and 3.

1.2   The Value-Free Approach

Charlotte Buhler distinguishes three histori-
cal trends in dealing with client values: the
first was begun by Freud and the early psychoanalysts; the second is exemplified by Rogers'
client-centered (non-directive) therapy; and the
third, a more recent view, is not tied to any
particular doctrine and gives therapists a
fairly free hand in bringing their own values
into the therapeutic situation.[2] Although Buhler
distinguishes Freud and Rogers as proponents of
different trends, I will show that they present
similar approaches and fail, if they fail at all,

4

for similar reasons. In this section I will describe the early analytic and Rogerian views which propose what I will call a "value-free" approach.

We should begin by noting that the value-free thesis does not maintain that client values should never be mentioned or dealt with in therapy. Heinz Hartmann, a persuasive analytic representative of this view, claims that knowledge of the patient's moral views is required for a therapist to completely understand the client.[3] This means that some of the client's values need to be discussed with the therapist. In fact, the client's recognition of his own values is part of the goal of therapy.[4]

If client values play an important role in therapy, what is it that should be eliminated? Hartmann claims that a therapist should not express his moral judgments of what the client says in therapy.[5] The therapist's values are "best kept in the background."[6] This is a realizable goal for the circumspect therapist.

Wilder, also an analyst, makes a similar claim:

> The generally accepted point of view has been that the therapist's values should be kept out of the therapeutic relationship.[7]

And Goldstein, a psychiatrist, says:

> it has often been demanded that psycho-therapy keep free from values . . . the therapist is not supposed to impose his own values upon the patient. . . .[8]

Proponents of the value-free thesis, then, intend that only the values of the therapist should be eliminated from therapy. One reason for this view, held by Hartmann and Freud, is a scientific model of therapy. Concluding his book, <u>Psycho-analysis and Moral Values</u>, Hartmann says:

> I did not try to adduce arguments for or
> against specific moral directions. I
> did not avoid this because I am blind to
> its importance, but because I realize
> it has no place in scientific discourse.
> It belongs not in the realm of science,
> but of ultimate personal positions; no
> scientific psychology, even if it were
> perfected beyond what it is today could
> take the place of personal responsibility
> in these matters.[9]

and

> Science cannot decide on what aims one
> ought to strive for, or what values
> should be considered supreme.[10]

There are two strands of reasoning here, the most prominent being the scientific nature of therapy: science is not in a position to make moral judgments about its ends. But in denying that therapy, qua science, can provide ultimate aims, he indicates that it is a person's <u>own responsibility</u> to supply these. This suggests that not only would it be a technical mistake to provide moral values and goals for the client, but would also constitute an infringement on the client's right to formulate his own moral beliefs.

Not only are the analyst's moral judgments restricted from analysis but also his philosophy of life or picture of the best life for man. Hartmann agrees with Freud that "Psychoanalysis is not . . . in a position to create a philosophy of life."[11] This leads Hartmann to worry about analysts who teach their own philosophies under the guise of teaching analysis.[12]

In describing the proper function of psychoanalysis, Hartmann compares it to technology.[13]

6

In his therapeutic work he [the therapist]
keeps other values in abeyance and concentrates on the realization of one category
of values only: health values.[14]

In Hartmann's view, and this characterizes the
value-free approach generally, it is possible to
promote these health values without taking a stand
on a philosophy of life or morality.

This puts the therapist in a difficult position. As mentioned above, he cannot help but
discuss the client's values. In fact many of the
client's problems are fraught with conflicts which
involve values. If the therapist should not guide
his patient, what should his role be? Once again,
Hartmann:

[The analyst's] attitude is that of the
psychological student of moral--and
other--valuations and their inter-
relation with other individual or social
psychological phenomena.[15]

In attempting to promote health, the client
is encouraged to take an active role in putting
his own principles and judgments into a workable
form. The therapist merely provides insight into
the relations between the values that the client
holds, and between the client's values and the
values of others (whether these be of other
individuals or groups). In restricting himself to
interpretation and clarification, the analyst
leaves the use of analytic insight up to the client.

In denying that moral imperatives can be
legitimately derived from psychoanalytic
findings, it might appear that I limit
radically the effects of analysis on
moral life. But . . . it is also true
that given a set of ultimate aims,
analysis has a significant potential for
clarifying and organizing them and, under
certain circumstances, also for helping

7

toward their realization.[16]

Hartmann's general view with respect to the values of clients is one of non-interference. The therapist provides the tools necessary for the client to work on his own values. The ultimate aims are not provided by analysis, but are provided by the client.[17] (How this statement fits in with his view that the therapist promotes "health values" above all others will be discussed more thoroughly in 1.3.1. This much is clear, however: health values must be given priority by the client as well. Otherwise, promoting health values would be to urge values not provided by the client.)

Szasz, also an analyst, holds a similar view. He states that it is not the analyst's place to encourage behavior of any type; this would restrict the freedom of the client.[18] The therapist is limited much as Hartmann claimed in that he must not direct the restructuring of the client's values nor should he influence the patient's decisions to act or not act on those values. Again we see the therapist described as a mere interpreter of the client's psychological data and no more. The goal of therapy is to educate the client "to liberate and fulfill his own nature, not to resemble others."[19] Hence, the client must be completely free in his use of analytic insight.[20] Violation of these restrictions constitutes both a technical and a moral mistake.[21]

Here we see Szasz presenting the same reasons as Hartmann for restricting the use of therapist values. Szasz holds that a therapist who utilizes his own values in therapy would be making a technical mistake; to do that would be to engage in some form of counseling, not analysis. That is, bringing therapist values in therapy is incompatible with the principles of psychoanalysis. But given his description of the goal of psychoanalysis as personal autonomy, which Szasz sees as an individual right, it would also be unethical

8

for a therapist to act in such a way.

Another example of the value-free thesis can be found in the early work of Carl Rogers. (This is what Buhler refers to as the "second trend.") The development of non-directive or client-centered therapy was an attempt to rely on the client's ability to help or heal himself.[22] As such, it implies that the therapist must keep out of the healing process; to intrude would inhibit the natural movement towards health that people exhibit. Hence, the more a therapist brings his perspectives into therapy, the longer and less effective therapy will be.

On this theory, what is the role of the therapist? Why is one needed? One could imagine an interpretation of non-directive therapy where the client would be better off without a therapist. Rogers would surely reject such an interpretation. To show this, I will examine why Rogers denies that a therapist should be passive. This will help explain what a therapist should do and why one is needed.

Rogers' main objection to a passive technique, that is, one which prescribes mere observation, is that it will very often convey an attitude of indifference.[23] It is a tenet of client-centered therapy (in the end a more appropriate description than "non-directive") that this attitude inhibits the growth and well being of the client. Even though he rejects passivity, Rogers does not adopt Hartmann's and Szasz's view of the therapist's role. He rejects their interpretive approach as "too intellectualistic, and if taken too literally, may focus the process in the counselor. It can mean that only the counselor knows what the feelings are, and if it acquires this meaning it becomes a subtle lack of respect for the client."[24]

The position that Rogers does prescribe for the therapist is "to assume insofar as he is able, the internal frame of reference of the client, to perceive the client himself as he is seen by himself, to lay aside all perceptions from the external frame of reference while doing so, and to communicate something of this empathetic understanding to the client."[25] Although Rogers sees the activity of the therapist differently from Hartmann and Szasz, he agrees with them about the status of the therapist's values. In another reference to the sometimes harmful influence a therapist can have, Rogers says:

> In client-centered therapy this problem has been minimized considerably by the very nature of the therapist's position . . . when evaluation of the client or of his expressions is almost nonexistent, counselor bias has little opportunity to become evident, or indeed to exist.[26]

This reflects Rogers' attitude about the abilities of the patient and the proper attitude of the therapist vis-á-vis those abilities. The therapist must be completely non-judgmental in his "empathetic identification" with a client. This, however, shows that this identification has certain limits. It is surely true that we all judge ourselves and our actions from time to time but the therapist does not assume this role of the client. The therapist is enjoined merely to interpret, albeit from the perspective of the client, and must restrict his judgment in order to allow the client to choose his own goals whether they be "social or anti-social, moral or immoral."[27]

All three therapists agree that it would be both a technical and a moral error to impose values on a client. Regarding the technical aspect, analysts hold that therapy should help clients integrate various conscious and unconscious facets of their personality. Hartmann claimed that values play an important role in this integration. It is unlikely that imposed values would aid the integrative process, since they may

10

not fit well with the client's personality. Szasz described the goal of therapy in terms of "freedom and autonomy." Whatever else he means by these terms it is clear that this goal requires that values should not be imposed in therapy. For Rogers, of course, value influence is likely to inhibit a client's natural movement toward health. We have already described the moral injunctions against imposing values on a client. Hartmann held that value development is a personal responsibility; Szasz, that a client has the right to determine his own values; Rogers, that value imposition would violate the dignity of the client.

Although Rogerian and psychoanalytic approaches to the problem of client value development are similar in the ways described, there are differences as well. For example, Freud suggested that a client may have to be pushed to think about problems that are being avoided.[28] This kind of influence, which would occur during analysis, would be rejected by Rogers. Sterba, another analyst, argues for the propriety of "post-analytic" influence. That is, a therapist is allowed to use "persuasion and threat, promise of reward, encouragement and praise."[29] This is justified when the client's values are stable and all that is needed is to get him to act on them. On Roger's view, this would violate the dignity of the client, which consists (at least in part) in the ability to act because one wants to, not because of force or pressure.

Although Rogers does not direct therapy as do Freud or Sterba, does this show that a Rogerian therapist is a technical, disinterested advisor, as Buhler suggests? As we saw above, the Rogerian therapist attempts to identify with the client, adopt the client's point of view. If a therapist can do this, he will not bring in his own values since he will have adopted the client's values. This sort of identification precludes detachment. In fact, it is hard to see how a therapist could be more involved. The mistake made by Buhler and others who interpret Rogers in this way is to conflate detachment with non-directiveness whereas Rogers' program is designed to achieve the latter by rejecting the former.

Rogers differs from the analysts only in the method by which non-client values are eliminated from therapy. The goal is the same: allow the client's values to develop independently of the influence of therapy.

The value-free thesis, then, is an attempt to protect both the principles on which a client bases moral judgments and the particular moral judgments of a client. This is not to say that client values should be excluded from therapy. Bolgar claims that the search for values is often the reason people seek therapy.[30] Buhler states that the development of a "hierarchy of values" is a question that often arises in therapy.[31] Jon Ehrenwald concurs: a therapist "must help the patient evolve and fortify a system of values which stands up to the criteria of reality testing."[32] The value-free thesis, then, is an attempt to deal with the need to help a client examine and restructure his values in a way that is healthy and that does not violate the rights of the client. Whether this is achieved by merely analyzing the client or by trying to "become" the client, both methods attempt to shield the client from the influence of the therapist's values. This is the point of restricting the therapist from talking about his values in the therapeutic process--a process, it is maintained, in which clients can become extremely vulnerable.

1.3   Examination of the Value-Free Approach

Buhler notes that dissatisfaction with the value-free approach has prompted some therapists to suggest that questions of influence should be left up to individual therapists, or that value influence is simply a part of therapy and is not a cause of concern.[33]

In 1.3.1-1.3.2 I will examine two arguments against the value-free approach. This will enable us to see, in 1.4, whether such arguments warrant dismissing or ignoring the problem of therapy's effect on client values.

The two arguments I will present to refute the value-free thesis are based on two ways in which the value-free thesis can be understood. These two interpretations are based on a distinction which can be found in the literature, but is not to my knowledge used in formulating the value-free thesis. A therapist can transmit (what I will call) "therapeutic values" and "therapist values." Therapeutic values are those which a therapist holds in virtue of subscribing to a particular theory of counseling. Therapist values are those to which a therapist subscribes independently of his official theory. There will very likely be both overlap and conflict between therapeutic and therapist values. Rogers claims that unless there is considerable overlap between therapeutic and therapist values, it will be very difficult for a person to learn and practice that therapy.[34] Although Rogers makes this point in the context of client-centered therapy, it seems a valid point about any therapy.

Buhler cites the conflict between these two sources of values as one of the major problems facing a therapist.

> He [the therapist] must clarify the
> position he himself wants to take with
> respect to the patient's value system
> and value considerations. Apart from
> this he must have come to terms with
> the values in the theory to which he
> subscribes and which may not in all
> respects correspond with his own feelings
> about things.[35]

And, quoting from an unpublished manuscript by Hedda Bolger:

13

. . . the therapist brings both his personal value system and the values of psychoanalysis into the psychoanalytic situation.[36]

On the basis of this distinction the value-free thesis can be interpreted in two ways:
   a) that therapeutic values ought to be excluded,
   b) that therapist values ought to be excluded.
The following two sections will attempt to show that neither of these goals can be reached. Since a value-free theorist would have to maintain at least one of them, this would appear to refute the value-free thesis.

1.3.1   Therapeutic Influence

No one denies that there is or should be therapeutic influence; without it there would be no point to therapy. The question, rather, concerns the nature of this influence: must therapeutic influence involve influencing the client's values? The value-free thesis maintains that therapeutic goals can be achieved without influencing or directing the client's value decisions. Opponents of this reading of the value-free thesis can argue in two related ways: they can either appeal to theories of therapy to show the values they contain, or they can analyze the nature of therapy to show that it is the kind of activity which must rely on values. To illustrate the first kind of argument, I will examine briefly the theories of Hartmann, Szasz and Rogers.

Hartmann clearly recognizes that therapy relies on values. He does not deny that health is a value[37] or that psychoanalysis aims at providing health as a value.[38] However, a problem arises if a client does not desire health. If such a person entered therapy, would not Hartmann be "imposing" health as a value? Szasz is similarl[y]

14

committed to the presence and communication of values in psychotherapy. He states that:

> [psychoanalysis] is a model of the human encounter regulated by the ethics of individualism and personal autonomy.[39]

and

> The ethic of the analytic relationship <u>is communicated</u> by what actually occurs between analyst and analysand.[40]
> (emphasis mine)

Although Szasz may avoid <u>saying</u> anything about values, he structures the therapist-client relationship to exemplify "the ethics of individualism."

Rogers is a little harder to pin down but he also sees therapy as involving <u>and</u> communicating a type of value, viz., the fundamental worth and dignity of the client as a person. This leads Patterson to claim that client-centered therapy rests on two principles:

a) each person is a person of worth in himself and is therefore to be respected as such,

b) each individual has the right of self-direction, to choose or select his own values and goals and to make his own decisions.[41]

It must be emphasized that not only do these principles underlie Rogerian therapy, but <u>that the client's adoption of them is part of the thera-peutic process.</u> This is effected by a calm acceptance of the client and what he presents in therapy.[42] Also, the very structure of Rogerian therapy is aimed at making this clear for the patient. (We saw this element in Szasz as well.)

Such illustrations are often used to show the implausibility of the value-free thesis.

However, there is still a possibility that other theories of therapy might not rely on values. To show the failure of the value-free thesis with respect to therapeutic influence, a more powerful argument is needed, one that shows that theories of therapy must rely on values. To show this we must ask what the point of theory is, what it attempts to achieve. A general, but true, answer is to help the client become as mentally healthy as possible. It is, therefore, a goal directed activity which aims at the good or well being of a client. But to aim at such a goal is to employ values in just the way value-free theorists want to avoid. This is because the goal must be described in terms of values which describe or put limits on what a good life is like. Since therapy attempts to get the client to achieve this goal and since this goal incorporates values, therapy attempts to get the client to adopt or believe in values.

In the wake of these arguments, we must wonder how Hartmann, Szasz, Rogers and others could maintain the value-free thesis. The answer, I think, is that the arguments that show the presence of values in therapy, especially the last one, are deceptively obvious. Once we understand that the goal of therapy can be very abstract and general, the value-free therapist has another option: he can stress the compatibility of therapeutic values with the various value systems clients might have.

To understand why this is a reasonable alternative we need to look at what therapeutic goals might include, and how their realization would affect decisions a person might make. Let us consider first how living up to an ideal life (a therapeutic goal) would affect the living of one's life. Hampshire's discussion of ethical ideals in Two Theories of Morality is helpful in this context since his remarks are sometimes more about the nature of ideals rather than ethical ideals. Although an ideal maps out a

16

preferred way to live one's life, it is not the kind of thing which can simply be imitated. Given the diversity of human capabilities, opportunities, and desires, there are an indefinite number of ways to live up to an ideal.[43] Suppose altruism were part of an ideal: this does not imply that there is some best way of being altruistic. Altruistic behavior can include everything from being a garbage collector to a doctor who gives up his wealthy clientele to help the poor. Another feature of an ideal is that it may include values that are incompatible in particular circumstances.[44] Suppose that the ideal includes self-interest and altruism, as surely any adequate ideal must. The question then arises as to which tendency should be given priority in the many cases where these conflict. It would seem impossible to give any general rule that one tendency should always override the other: there are some cases where self-interest should dominate, some where altruism should dominate and many unclear cases between. It is unlikely that we could simply "live up" to an ideal, copy it, since there are bound to be cases where we will have to choose between different aspects of that ideal. Thus there is good reason to agree with Hampshire when he says: "that there should be an abstract ethical ideal, the good for men in general is not inconsistent with there being great diversity in preferred ways of life, even among men living at the same place and time."[45]

The values incorporated in a theory of therapy would have to be abstract and general if that theory is to be effective with the wide range of people who enter therapy. So value-free theorists could admit, as they often do, that therapeutic goals involve values without blatantly contradicting themselves. This is because of the possibility that therapeutic values are so basic and general that they can form the basis of any value system.

In 1.3.1.1 I will argue that although these values are general, there is no reason to suppose

that they comport with all possible value systems.
I will further argue that the kind of value
influence I have been describing as therapeutic
would be a factor in therapy even if these values
need not be included in a theory of therapy.

1.3.1.1   The Generality of Therapeutic Values

We have seen that therapy is an activity that
endeavors to help clients change for the better.
The general argument for the presence of values in
therapy was that only such beliefs can give an
interpretation of "better." We must now see if a
concept of mental health, and hence the therapy
based on it, will comport with the range of
values that clients might hold.

Hartmann's position was clear: when psychoanalysis is handled correctly, it need take no
position on a philosophy of life or moral values.
I will consider the position he takes on a
philosophy of life first. It is not completely
clear what he means by that phrase, but since he
sometimes contrasts it with "moral values," I
will take it to refer to non-moral preferences
dealing with major aspects of one's life.
Examples might be aesthetic ideals, decisions
about whom to marry and vocational planning. If
this is what Hartmann had in mind, then he has
his case; it seems unlikely that a counseling
theory would need to take a stand on such issues.
In fact, the generality that is required of such
a theory would preclude it from taking a stand on
particular issues.

Beyond resolving particular dilemmas, however,
there exist criteria which we use to solve them
and, more fundamentally, the ways in which we
analyze problems in the first place. It would be
in these areas that therapy would have an influence
Hartmann recognizes this:

        Some philosophies of life will find it
        easier than others to make use of the

> picture of man it [psychoanalysis]
> presents. Every strictly dogmatic
> attitude, every taboo against psycho-
> logical insight, and particularly
> [taboos] against objective studies of
> instinctual matters will limit readiness
> to learn from psychoanalysis.[46]

Hartmann is understating his case. Unless a
therapist can persuade a client to change or at
least suspend those beliefs, psychoanalysis
cannot take place. This will hold true for any
client who holds beliefs fundamentally opposed
to those central to the therapist's theory. The
conflict just described concerns a general approach
to problems. The approach one does take would
seem to constitute a significant part of one's
philosophy of life. In fact, the most recent
quoted passage suggests a principle that one
person has claimed underlies every theory of
counseling (except, perhaps, strict behavioral
therapy), the principle of "thinking things
through."[47] This would mean that anyone who
preferred "instinctual" or "impulsive" reactions
would have problem solving modes directly opposed
to the kind presented in most therapies. (Even
in behavioral therapy one must decide what the
problem is before prescribing remedies for that
problem. The concern is then with the process by
which that decision is made.)

Many types of therapy, then, urge a certain
approach to the problems of life, a reflective
approach. Of course, there could be theories
that urge just the opposite: act on impulse, your
first thoughts are your best, etc. Further, a
theory could urge reflection in some instances
and impulse in others (perhaps a more realistic
approach). This is not an objection to the
present point, however, which is a general one:
a theory of counseling must employ some mode of
problem solving--the client is there to solve
his problems--and this will reflect a fundamental
belief about the best way to go about directing
one's life.

19

We have just seen that part of the goal of
therapy is to get the patient to employ certain
problem solving modes. Another aspect of a
therapeutic goal, one which may have more immediate
and drastic consequences for the client, concerns
the criteria on which decisions are made. That
is, besides offering a mode of problem solving,
such as reflection, there must be some criteria
which are used to evaluate the possibilities which
are being reflectively considered.

Irving Yalom, author of The Theory and Practice
of Group Psychotherapy, and Thomas Szasz differ in
a way that clarifies the issue. Yalom suggests
certain conditions that would allow (obligate?) a
therapist to terminate therapy with a client even
though the therapist feels that a continuation of
therapy would help the client progress. In a
particular case, Yalom feared that his client
would "outgrow" his spouse, creating new problems
for the client.[48] In this passage and others,
Yalom makes it clear that he is concerned with
the well-being and happiness of his clients; he
implies that it is better to get along with what
one has (at least in some cases) than to achieve
the psychological maturity of which one is
capable.

It should come as no surprise that Szasz
would strongly oppose a therapist making the
decision to terminate, at least on these grounds.
Szasz's therapeutic goal, client autonomy,
dictates that "it is more important that the
patient be free to choose than that he choose to
be healthy, wealthy or wise."[49] Again, "The aim
of therapy is not to achieve 'happiness' or even
'well being,' but to learn about one's self and
develop personal autonomy."[50] These and similar
considerations lead Szasz to claim that "the
analyst has no right to terminate the analysis.
This is not his job; it is the patient's."[51]

One might object to drawing any conclusions
about therapy on the basis of the above conflict

since it is clear that Yalom and Szasz practice very different therapies. Although their techniques and goals are very different, my point still stands: the goal of therapy will reflect a philosophy of life. The reason for comparing Yalom and Szasz was not to suggest that all therapies are identical, but to show that what distinguishes them, in part, are divergent conceptions of what a good life is like. The Yalom/Szasz comparison showed that they did have different ideas of the good life and how that difference can manifest itself in the client-therapist relationship.

I have shown how therapy must rely on non-moral beliefs about the best life for man.[52] Next, we need to ask if a theory of counseling can escape moral beliefs or principles. Once again, it is unlikely that a theory would take a stand on specific issues such as premarital sex, cheating on tests or the like. More general aspects of morality must be considered if we are to find them embedded in a theory of counseling.

Let us look again at the goal of therapy, viz., the mental health of the client. The next question that usually arises concerns the particular conception of mental health being talked about. Right now, however, all we need to ask is what kinds of things should a definition of mental health include, that is, how should one go about formulating it? One way to describe mental health is in terms of healthy responses to the various things one encounters. Since much of what a person has to cope with are his own and others' moral codes, part of being mentally healthy will include healthy reactions to moral mandates and restrictions. The argument I am going to present now will show that how this healthy response is construed represents a moral stance that will be reflected in the therapeutic process.

I will begin by considering Freud's attempt to show that moral beliefs are _merely_ a product of

21

identification and internalization.[53]   If a
therapist held to Freud's view, then that would
surely affect the way he would advise a client
whose problems arose from conflicts with moral
restrictions.   Such a therapist would "urge"
(though not in so many words--we will see in
1.3.2 how this might occur without the therapist
or the client being aware of it) the client to
take the moral issues less seriously.   In other
words, metaethical beliefs can have a direct
effect on how a therapist directs therapy.

   This particular issue is at the heart of
some objections that O. H. Mowrer has to traditional (pre-ego-psychology) psychoanalysis.
Mowrer does not disagree with the general picture
of man that Freud proposes--id, ego, super-ego--
but rather with Freud's conception of what counts
as a healthy integration of these forces.   Mowrer
interprets the Freudian conception of neurosis as
involving an overly harsh super-ego.   The ego
takes these demands as law and represses the id,
resulting in guilt and anxiety.   The remedy to
this problem is to reduce the severity of the
super-ego's demands.   But since the super-ego is
the seat of moral values, Mowrer sees the Freudian
approach as degrading the importance of morality
in a healthy individual, introducing the possibility of therapeutically induced sociopathy or
egoism.[54]   Mowrer does not deny that Freudian
therapy would tend to remove felt anxiety and
guilt, but only that this is not the best way to
achieve this goal.[55]   In Mowrer's scheme the super-
ego demands are often realistic, and the Freudian
approach "reality distorting."   Mowrer suggests
that the proper way to ease anxiety or guilt is
not by reducing the efficacy of the super-ego, but
by increasing the strength of the ego, enabling
the person to meet his super-ego demands, not
ignore them.[56]   In other words, neurosis does not
stem from an overly harsh super-ego, but from an
ego which is too weak to resist the id.

   It is not my task to settle this issue,
although it does seem that there is truth on both

22

sides. Mowrer, in fact, admits that Freudian style neurosis could occur.[57] Still, it seems improbable that all or even most of one's super-ego demands are reasonable or unreasonable. In fact, the reasonableness of such demands seems to be one of the major problems that people face. Max W. Friedmann makes roughly the same comment:

> Mowrer has recently emphasized the importance of supporting the super-ego instead of the id. He overlooked, however . . . the necessity to destroy first the false super-ego structures in order to set free vital desires, before the building up of real moral values.[58]

The same kind of qualification that was made about the Yalom/Szasz conflict needs to be made here, viz., that I am using Freud and Mowrer to illustrate the point that a concept of morality will guide one's formulation of a concept of mental health. Hence, to argue that ego-psychology avoids this problem by placing the seat of true morality in the ego is not relevant. Once this maneuver has been made we still need to know the criteria by which "true morality" is identified, and we are back to the same problem which faced Freud and Mowrer: how do we tell true or healthy moral stances from the false ones? Resolving this issue will require the adoption of some moral criteria.

I have tried to argue that a complete theory of counseling will be based on moral and non-moral principles about the best life for a human being. Although principles may admit of much diversity, there is no reason to think that therapeutic values will comport with the indefinite number of ways personal value systems might be constructed. Since it is absurd to suggest eliminating therapeutic influence, and since therapeutic influence involves value influence, one reading of the value-free thesis, that theories of counseling not include values, must fail.

Before turning to the problem of therapist influence, it will be useful to consider the possibility that my arguments for the presence of values in theories of therapy are defective. Suppose someone objected that I pack too much into a theory of therapy, that a theory of therapy could contain one simple injunction: reduce client anxiety.   Although this may not be a very good theory, our objector might continue, it is none the less a theory: a person could conceivably conduct therapy on the basis of it.   On this view a therapist is similar to a building contractor: if the client wants the service, that is fine; if not, that is fine too.   If we allow our objector that such a minimal theory would still count as a theory, would that mean therapeutic influence need not take place?   I think not.   It must be remembered that anxiety is the result of a conflict between two or more of a client's beliefs, or between the client's beliefs and the beliefs of others.   Clearly, resolving this conflict will require some stand on what beliefs to put first. This will be true of every attempt to solve a problem: there must be some way to decide between the various solutions.   Hence, problems that involv values do not admit of value-free decision.   Whatever course is chosen will reflect some priority of values.

Buhler cites a case that exemplifies this kind of problem.   A woman, suffering from a great deal of anxiety and fear, decided to endure it rather than be healthy.   The client (and Buhler) felt the anxiety stemmed from the inability to live up to certain religious convictions.   Since Buhler judged that the woman's religious convictions were an integral part of her personality, Buhler decided not to meddle with them.   Instead, she tried to work within the woman's religious framework.[59]   This is a clear case where the neutral goal of anxiety reduction could have great effects on a client's values.

Although certain attempts at anxiety reduction in the case above would result in value

24

influence, was Buhler's approach neutral? There is reason to think that it was not. The role of the therapist is to help the client <u>find</u> and <u>define</u> the cause of problems. On this assumption, the failure of the therapist to work on an area that is related to the problem could reasonably be taken as indicating that the therapist judges those areas not to be problematic. Hence, the client could interpret the therapist's behavior as approval of these beliefs, at least insofar as they relate to the client's current problem.

What I take this to show is that if values are not included in a theory of therapy, the therapist will provide them. This is because therapy is a goal directed activity which must employ some notion of the good life. The arguments I presented in this section to show the presence of values in theories of therapy were not merely meant to show what theories include, but were an attempt to shed light on the <u>nature</u> of therapy. The point is that therapy is a certain sort of activity and hence its theory should have certain features. If we remove these features from the theory, they will have to come from somewhere else. But, no matter where these values originate, they will be the kind of values I discussed under the rubric of therapeutic influence.

1.3.2 Therapist Influence

In the last two sections I showed that therapeutic value influence cannot be excluded from therapy. In the face of this a value-free theorist could retreat to a weaker thesis, viz., merely excluding therapist values. A value-free theorist could reasonably hold that the generality of therapeutic values makes them relatively harmless, since those who do not agree to them are not likely to enter therapy in the first place and, if they do, are not likely to be changed by therapy. As Hartmann has suggested, clients must share some basic views with a therapist if therapy

is to take place.[60] What must be avoided, on
this weaker view, is the client being influenced
by the personal values of the therapist. Unlike
therapeutic values, therapist values can be very
specific, such as beliefs that pre-marital sex is
immoral or even that facial hair is unsanitary or
unsightly. Since therapist values can be specific,
this influence can be very direct and harmful if
it blatantly conflicts with the client's values.
Unfortunately, it seems that therapist value
influence is as inescapable as therapeutic value
influence. Research indicates that it is impossible for a therapist to discuss material presented
by a client without revealing his personal values.
One study tested the change in moral beliefs of
psycho-therapeutic clients: the clients who
improved showed a tendency to develop moral
values held by their therapist.[61] Of course, it
is possible that this change was not due to an
uncritical acceptance of the therapist's views.
Another study, however, indicates a direct connection between the beliefs developed by the client
and those held by the therapist. In this latter
test therapists were able to manipulate a client's
behavior without the client's knowledge.[62] These
studies lead Patterson to say:

> . . . it is easy to imagine the effect
> on the client of such responses of the
> therapist to the patient's verbalization
> as a trace of a smile or a pleased look,
> an incipient nod of the head, or other
> mechanisms, indicating his attitude,
> favorable or unfavorable toward the
> patient's production--all of which may
> be unknown to the therapist and the
> patient.[63]

So, the program of getting a therapist to
keep his personal values out of therapy is bound
to fail, since he cannot guard against the many
ways such values can be expressed. This is not
the only problem with excluding therapist
values.

C. Knight Aldrich convincingly argues that a therapist who just "goes along" with a client is not avoiding risk. He refers to a case where the reluctance of a therapist to comment on a client's somewhat unusual behavior was understood as "permission, sanction, and even encouragement."[64]

This puts the value-free thesis in a very difficult position. The goal of the thesis was to protect the patient from being morally indoctrinated by a therapist. Unfortunately, enjoining the therapist not to express values runs two related risks: that the client will adopt the values anyway and that values may be "conveyed" that the therapist does not hold. In other words, the program to minimize value influence (whether these have therapeutic or therapist origins) by enjoining the therapist to keep non-client values out of therapy will not do the job it was intended to do.

1.4 Conclusion

In this chapter I have tried to do several things. First I suggested that imposing values on a client is a common worry among therapists. I then examined the first major attempt to deal with this problem, the value-free thesis, which proposed the elimination of all sources of values that did not originate in the client. Two non-client sources of values were identified: the theory of counseling and the therapist's personal convictions. I argued that a theory of counseling must ultimately rest on values and then used studies of the client/therapist relationship to show that it would be impossible, and in some cases harmful, for a therapist to keep his personal convictions in abeyance.

We must be careful, however, about how we interpret these results. Buhler, in the wake of such arguments, wonders:

Do we have to leave this fundamental question of influences exercised on a patient to the decisions and wisdom of the individual therapist? Sterba resigns himself to this necessity; Patterson does not see a problem necessarily arising from the question being left in the hands of the individual analyst nor do Ginsburg and the previously quoted discussants of his paper. I, personally, have always felt that this question of influences is a tremendous problem. . . .[65]

Buhler's intuitions are well founded. None of the arguments presented above go even part of the way towards suggesting that therapeutic or therapist value influence is unimportant or that its control should be left to individual therapists.

This is evident if we attend to the goal of the value-free thesis, viz., preventing an uncritical adoption of values by the client. As a means to that end, the value-free thesis tried to eliminate non-client values. Critics of this approach show, as I did in 1.3.1-1.3.2, that this way of handling the problem is fraught with theoretical and technical problems. None of this, however, shows that the original goal should be abandoned or that its importance should be left to the personal opinions of therapists. To say that certain values cannot be eliminated from therapy is not to say that we need no longer worry about value imposition. On the contrary, this makes finding a solution to the problem all the more important. Buhler states her aim as finding some middle ground between "leaving the patient to find his own values himself and the other extreme of actively inducing beliefs in him."[66] What I take this chapter to show is that a solution to this problem must come to terms with the therapeutic situation as it is: an encounter whose emphasis is often on just those aspects that the value-free thesis wanted to eliminate.

In the next chapter I will argue that any attempt to solve the problem we have been discussing must first offer a more succinct analysis of the problem. I will attempt to do this by discussing the problem of indoctrination. This will help us identify the problem which client value adoption presents for therapy. It will become clear that how we describe the problem of client value adoption in therapy, and the importance we attach to it, will depend on our theory of value acquisition. The rest of Chapter 2 will be devoted to discussions of two major theories of value acquisition. In Chapter 3 I will argue that the more viable theory of moral acquisition presents a solution to the problem of a client adopting values in therapy. This solution will focus on therapy as a place where people go when they are unable to plan and deliberate about their lives. If we concentrate on the process of deliberation, we will see why therapeutic and therapist influence, even if explicit and direct, need not be construed as imposing values on a client.

Notes

[1] William Frankena, "Value and Valuation," p. 229.

[2] Charlotte Buhler, Values in Psychotherapy, p. 7.

[3] Heinz Hartmann, Psychoanalysis and Moral Values, p. 39.

[4] Ibid., p. 37.

[5] Ibid., p. 54.

[6] Ibid.

[7] Joseph Wilder, quoted in C. H. Patterson, Counseling and Psychotherapy, p. 53.

[8] Kurt Goldstein, "Health as a Value," p. 183.

[9] Hartmann, p. 102.

[10] Ibid., p. 51.

[11] Sigmund Freud, quoted in Hartmann, p. 20.

[12] Hartmann, pp. 23-24.

[13] Ibid., pp. 20-21.

[14] Ibid., p. 55.

[15] Ibid., p. 10.

[16] Ibid., p. 85.

[17] Ibid., p. 62.

[18] Thomas Szasz, The Ethics of Psychoanalysis, pp. 16, 18-19, 23, 24, 75, 103.

[19] Ibid., p. 1.

[20] Ibid., p. 24.

[21] Ibid., pp. 24, 51, 75, 135, 180.

[22] Carl Rogers, Client Centered Therapy, pp. 14, 22-23.

[23] Ibid., p. 27.

[24] Ibid.

[25] Ibid., p. 29.

[26] Ibid., p. 42.

[27] Ibid., p. 48.

[28] Sigmund Freud, quoted in Buhler, pp. 7-8.

[29] Richard Sterba, quoted in Buhler, p. 196.

[30] Hedda Bolger, quoted in Buhler, p. 10.

[31] Ibid., p. 123.

[32] Jon Ehrenwald, quoted in Buhler, p. 11.

[33] Ibid., pp. 12, 19, 197.

[34] Rogers, pp. 20-21.

[35] Buhler, p. 196.

[36] Hedda Bolger, quoted in Buhler, p. 10.

[37] Hartmann, p. 73.

[38] Ibid., p. 55.

[39] Szasz, p. 17.

[40] Ibid., p. 24.

[41]C. H. Patterson, _Counseling and Psychotherapy_, p. 57.

[42]Rogers, p. 194.

[43]Stuart Hampshire, _Two Theories of Morality_, pp. 43, 50.

[44]Ibid., p. 42.

[45]Ibid., p. 48.

[46]Hartmann, p. 62.

[47]Rudolf Ekstein, quoted in Buhler, p. 28.

[48]Irving Yalom, _The Theory and Practice of Group Psychotherapy_, p. 369.

[49]Szasz, p. 48.

[50]Ibid., p. 186.

[51]Ibid., p. 138.

[52]I am not going to argue, as one might, that to urge a method of problem solving or a goal such as happiness is to put forward a moral view. Although this could be attempted, I am afraid that it might confuse more than it clarifies; hence, I will admit the moral/non-moral distinction. This is not to deny that the way these non-moral factors are handled may have moral ramifications. Surely Szasz would judge Yalom's principles of termination as violating the rights of the client. But, even if Szasz is correct, this does not show that the goal of happiness is immoral.

[53]Sigmund Freud, _Civilization and Its Discontents_ (especially Chapters III and IV), and _The Ego and the Id_ (especially Chapter III).

[54]O. H. Mowrer, "New Evidence Concerning the Nature of Psychopathology," p. 142.
32

[55] Ibid., p. 142.

[56] Ibid., p. 145.

[57] Ibid., p. 141.

[58] Max W. Friedmann, comment on "Values and Their Relationship to Psychiatric Principles and Practice," p. 573.

[59] Buhler, pp. 138-145.

[60] Hartmann, p. 62.

[61] Patterson, p. 67.

[62] Ibid., p. 68.

[63] Ibid.

[64] S. W. Standal and R. S. Corsini, Critical Incidents in Psychotherapy, p. 31.

[65] Buhler, p. 19.

[66] Ibid., p. 6.

CHAPTER 2

COGNITIVE AND NON-COGNITIVE APPROACHES TO
MORALITY AND MORAL ACQUISITION

2.0 Introduction

In the last chapter I showed that the limitations of the value-free thesis did not in themselves vitiate the goal of preventing the client
from arbitrarily adopting therapeutic and
therapist values. We saw that there were both
therapeutic and ethical reasons to support that
goal. In this chapter I will attempt to specify
the problem therapists face in discussing values
with clients. This will enable us to identify the
factors which underlie this problem. We will see
that a major obstacle to solving the problem of
value adoption in therapy is that there is no
clear notion of the problem or what a solution to
it must be like.

If we look back to Chapter 1 and examine the
worries of Hartmann, Rogers and Szasz, we see
that they all wanted to prevent one thing: value
indoctrination. They argued that there are two
reasons to avoid indoctrination:

a)   It is not the point of therapy to
     indoctrinate a client (it would be a
     technical error).

b)   It violates the rights of the client
     (a moral error).

These considerations show that there is more
at stake than understanding the effect of therapy
on a client's values. How a client's values are
affected is a problem that strikes at the very
heart of therapy. If a client's values change in
the course of therapy, and that change can be
explained only in terms of indoctrination, then

34

therapy (as we normally think of it) has not taken place. Therapy would have to be explained as an enterprise in which one person, a therapist, knowingly or unknowingly imposes his values on another, the client. As we have seen, this is incompatible with therapy. Since successful therapy often results in clients altering their values our conception of therapy would have to be altered radically.

In order to see if indoctrination is inevitable, we must first understand what we mean by 'indoctrination'. This will be the subject of 2.1. I conclude there that we cannot decide the issue of indoctrination independently of a conception of moral learning. In 2.2 I examine the analytic views of morality and moral learning and conclude that the psychoanalytic non-cognitive view makes the problem insoluble. In 2.3 I examine Kohlberg's theory of moral development, which is preferable to the non-cognitive view in many ways. Since that theory views moral development as a cognitive process, it overcomes the problems of the psychoanalytic view. Unfortunately, other aspects of Kohlberg's theory are unsatisfactory. The result is that indoctrination (or a similar difficulty) is still a problem. Finally, in 2.4 I suggest that Kohlberg is mistaken about some critical issues, especially indoctrination. This last issue forms the basis of Chapter 3.

2.1 Indoctrination

Indoctrination is one way to indicate the problem a therapist faces by helping structure a client's beliefs. We have argued that a therapist should not indoctrinate his clients, for ethical and practical reasons. But what is indoctrination? There is a great deal of literature on this topic, especially in the field of education. I will limit our discussion of indoctrination to aspects which are relevant to our topic.

35

In order to explain the nature of indoctrination, I will first offer three analyses which will be rejected. Understanding why these analyses fail will lead to a more plausible explanation.[67]

One way to understand indoctrination is in terms of the effect on the person indoctrinated.[68] That is, we tend to think of an indoctrinated individual holding steadfastly to beliefs, no matter how good the arguments that refute those beliefs may be. Although it may be true to say that an indoctrinated individual behaves this way, this does not help us understand what indoctrination is. It simply points out what happens when indoctrination is successful. But indoctrination is something that can be unsuccessful, too.[69] Since one can attempt to indoctrinate and fail, it is clear that this analysis is inadequate. Another problem with analyzing indoctrination by its effect is that a person does not have to be indoctrinated to act in ways we associate with indoctrination. A person could come to "blindly believe" something for many reasons.[70]

Another attempt to analyze indoctrination is by the type of material being indoctrinated.[71] This is plausible because indoctrination is usually thought of in terms of religious, political or moral doctrines. I. A. Snook points out that we do not think that grammar, for example, is the kind of thing that can be indoctrinated.[72] As natural as this analysis seems, there are possible examples of indoctrination that do not fit this pattern. If a political ideology was committed to a peculiar interpretation of biology, then it seems that we could talk about how these biological views might be indoctrinated.[73] One could reply that in this case it is really the political ideology that is being indoctrinated, or that we can talk about indoctrinating biology in this instance only because it is associated with a political ideology. There is, however, a more telling objection to analyzing indoctrination in terms of content, viz., this analysis rules out

36

teaching these types of issues in non-doctrinaire ways. This would imply that every class in religion, political theory or ethics would be indoctrinative. Although one might want to <u>argue</u> for this extreme position, a definition or analysis of 'indoctrination' is incapable of supporting such a strong claim. Hence, to explain indoctrination in terms of content fails: there can be cases of indoctrination that do not involve moral, political or religious doctrines, and further, it would definitionally exclude non-doctrinaire teaching in these areas.

A third way to analyze indoctrination is in terms of technique. Indoctrination is often associated with drill, reinforcement, threats and in general by a lack of reason giving.[74] Snook convincingly argues however, that successful indoctrination requires that a student be able to justify his beliefs to himself and others. Hence, the method of indoctrination may proceed by giving plenty of reasons for the beliefs which are being indoctrinated.

Showing that a method of indoctrination may make use of reasons leads to a further problem: how can we distinguish doctrinaire from non-doctrinaire teaching? Snook's answer is that indoctrination attempts to instill beliefs regardless of the reasons given for those beliefs. The reasons that an indoctrinator provides for his position are used <u>merely</u> as rhetorical devices. Hence, a "good reason" for an indoctrinator is one that is most likely to gain the support of the student, not the reason that really supports the belief. Non-indoctrinative teaching, on the other hand, emphasizes reasons for beliefs. Finally, it should be noted that "good intentions" are not incompatible with indoctrination. One could attempt to help another by indoctrinating certain beliefs. These considerations lead Snook to propose the following analysis of indoctrina-tion:

> A person indoctrinates P (a proposition
> or set of propositions) if he teaches
> with the intention that the pupil or
> pupils believe P regardless of the
> evidence.[75]

How will this analysis of indoctrination help
clarify the problems of therapy? For one thing,
it seems unlikely that therapists intend to instill
beliefs regardless of the reasons for those
beliefs. I will assume that therapists generally
have reasons for the views they express in therapy
such that they would not express these views if
they could be convinced that their reasons were
not good. This is not to say that therapists
are merely well-intentioned, it is to say that
therapists intend to not indoctrinate. Snook's
analysis of indoctrination, then, shows that it
can never be correct to describe a therapist as
morally indoctrinating if that therapist intends
to make the reasons for the moral views he presents
more important than the moral views themselves.

Does this show that therapists do not
encounter the problem I have been discussing? Of
course not; it merely points out that the problem
is not primarily one of indoctrination. We can
better understand our therapeutic problem if we
re-examine the analysis of indoctrination in
terms of the effect on the person indoctrinated.
Although this analysis was rejected, one of the
reasons for rejecting it is pertinent here, viz.,
the possibility that a person could act in ways
we associate with being indoctrinated without
being indoctrinated. This must surely happen in
therapy and education. Imagine a history class
studying World War II. In the course of this
class a student becomes a fanatical Nazi, although
the Nazi ideals were not promoted in any way.
Surely the teacher is not responsible for this; we
look for the cause in the student. What are the
reasons for his susceptibility to Nazi ideology?
We do not hold a teacher responsible for this
because such behavior is aberrant. No teacher or
school can be expected to teach material according

to in-depth psychological profiles of the students. They must, of course, take common, well-known psychological traits into account, and would be responsible if disastrous results occurred by ignoring these general human tendencies.

The above discussion points to a crucial difference between a teacher and therapist (although in some other ways they are similar).[76] A therapist is responsible if a client adopts views in therapy in a way that a teacher is not responsible for student belief acquisition. This does not mean that we can hold a therapist responsible for everything that occurs in therapy. Surely many things are beyond his control. We can still maintain, though, that the therapist should gauge his responses in therapy to the particular psychological profile of the client. Consider a client who harbors a strong irrational hatred for his brother. If a therapist ignored this in his responses to the client, and recklessly asked questions and made suggestions that reinforced this hatred, we could certainly hold the therapist responsible for the increased feelings of hatred that the client is likely to experience. A teacher, on the other hand, who went into detail about the enmity and rivalry between two brothers (in literature, or history, say) could produce the same effect. We would not, however, hold the teacher responsible. It is not part of a teacher's job, nor could it be, to guard against this kind of problem.

A therapist, then, is in a special position. His job presupposes that he have certain kinds of knowledge about a client's psychological make-up. He must be aware of this as he directs therapy, and, to an extent he is responsible if the client or others suffer as a result of his ignoring this.

The problem therapists face, then, is not the problem of indoctrination, but it is one that bears a close resemblance to it. A major objection to indoctrination is that this process is just as effective with true as well as false beliefs. That is, to say that a person is indoctrinated is to say nothing about the status of the beliefs that have been inculcated. This also seems to be the major objection to a client uncritically adopting the moral views expressed by the therapist. This type of belief adoption does not discriminate between true or false, good or bad, helpful or unhelpful beliefs. The real and legitimate fear that therapists have, then, is this: uncritical adoption of beliefs (whether in therapy or not) is likely to lead to the formation of a chaotic, and hence, inadequate system of beliefs.

Consider a person who believes he should be loyal to friends and help others (when helping poses no great inconvenience). If such a person tries to help another, but is urged by a friend not to help, what is he to do? If he helps, he is being disloyal; if he does not help, he is violating his belief that he should help others. If the beliefs have been adopted uncritically he will very likely have no way to resolve the tension, and may feel guilty no matter what he does. If, however, he bases one belief on the other, there would be a way to resolve this problem. Suppose the person believes that one should be loyal to friends on the ground that people should, in general, help one another. Being loyal to friends could be seen as a way in which people help each other: giving emotional support, helping with tasks that require more than one person, etc. One problem with uncritical value adoption, then, is that it provides no way to resolve value conflicts. Also, it gives a person no way to cope with novel situations, since there is no way to generate a principle which would apply. Being faced with a situation in which one must act, but for which one has no way to decide what should be done, is surely unsettling. Therapy, then, can be seen as an activity which often attempts to help clients straighten out their chaotic belief systems. Uncritical adoption of beliefs is many times a propensity that a client must learn to overcome; to allow it to continue in therapy is merely to complicate a problem a client may need to solve.

We can now sort out some ambiguities in Chapter 1. Throughout that chapter and the beginning of this one, I talked about the "problem of therapy" or the "problem presented by therapeutic and therapist values." This problem was variously described as "influencing a client's values," "unduly influencing a client's values," and "indoctrinating values." From now on, unless otherwise indicated, when I refer to the problem of therapy, or the problem of values in therapy, I mean the following:

> the impossibility of designing therapy in a way that will effectively prevent clients from uncritically adopting the values expressed in therapy (whether the values have therapeutic or therapist origins).

The therapeutic reasons for preventing uncritical adoption of values are those discussed in 1.2. But are the ethical objections discussed earlier still relevant? On our present conception it seems not; we envision the therapist as doing everything possible not to usurp the responsibility, infringe on the freedom, or violate the dignity of the client, insofar as he does not intend to impose any values on the client. There is, however, a further ethical problem. If a therapist has good reason to believe that a client may adopt therapeutic and therapist values no matter what precautions are taken, and that this is not likely to promote health, then therapy is potentially harmful. The ethical worry, then, is that a therapist might harm the client.

In order to evaluate the practical and ethical impact of uncritical adoption of values in therapy seriously, we need to understand how people come to adopt values and why they maintain them. For my purposes, I will concentrate on moral values (leaving a brief discussion of non-moral values till the end of the concluding chapter). I will argue that an important reason why psychoanalysts are unable to deal adequately with this problem is that they maintain naive views of morality and moral learning. A better understanding of morality and moral learning will shed a more helpful light on the problem of moral change in therapeutic clients.

2.2 Non-cognitive Conceptions of Morality and Moral Acquisition

In this section I will explain why therapists (especially analysts) fear that a client will uncritically adopt values expressed in therapy. We will see that if the analysts are correct about the nature of morality and the mode of its adoption, uncritical adoption of values in therapy is a problem which cannot be solved. As we have seen, the failure to solve this problem is a serious threat to therapy: it is not the point of therapy to have clients uncritically adopt material presented in therapy. The psychoanalytic theory of morality and moral acquisition, therefore, eliminates the possibility of therapy, at least in the way that many therapists conceive of it.

The theory of personality developed by Freud, and adopted by many (including non-analytic) therapists, posits three components of personality: the id, the ego and the super-ego.[77] The id is non-rational and attempts to gratify all its impulses.[78] As a child begins to interact with the environment, it becomes evident that not all desires can be gratified and that they must be organized in a way most suited to obtain pleasure. It is this necessity of coping with an unfriendly environment that brings about the development of the ego. On Freud's theory, the ego develops out of, is differentiated from, the id.[79] The id seeks pleasure and the ego's function is to

42

organize and cope with the environment in the way most suited to obtaining pleasure.

There are different things which can inhibit pleasure seeking. Some things, like physical barriers (e.g., the doorknob is too high, the cookies are out of reach), solve themselves, so to speak, as one grows. Some restrictions, however, are not so easily overcome, especially the moral restrictions, prohibitions, and orders given by one's parents and society. When the child first becomes aware of what he should and should not do, he treats these restrictions in the way he treats other barriers to pleasure, he tries to overcome them: to reach the doorknob he may stand on a box, to eat the forbidden candy he will wait until no one is looking. Eventually, however, these parental and social restrictions take on a special significance. Through the process of identification a child adopts the values of those around him and develops a super-ego.[80] The development of a super-ego is the result of internalizing the standards of an authority figure. This internalization "splits" the ego into two functions: the original ego, and the super-ego which watches over the ego in the way that a parent watches over a child.[81] Freud says that the super-ego "by giving permanent expression to the influence of the parents . . . perpetuates the existence of the factors to which it owes its origins."[82] One's moral values, then, are the results of internalizing the moral values of authority figures. This makes it sound as if we are limited to the values of our parents. Freud, however, did not think we are limited in this way; he had to explain the influence of society. Freud makes room for non-parental super-ego influence in the following way:

> [The super-ego] preserves throughout its life the character given to it by its derivation from the father-complex, namely, the capacity to stand apart from the ego and to rule it.[83] (emphasis mine)

43

Here the super-ego is defined <u>functionally</u>, not in terms of the content internalized from our primary parental identification. Once a person has a super-ego, he has the capacity (tendency?) to internalize values he finds outside the family. Freud traces this development as follows:

> What prompted the subject to form an ego-ideal . . . arose from the critical influence of his parents, to whom were added . . . those who trained and taught him and the innumerable and indefinable host of all the other people in his environment--his fellow-men--and public opinion.[84]

The general picture of moral acquisition is this: a child, through identification with an authority figure, develops the ability to criticize himself. The standards of this criticism are those that are passed on by the parents. As the child grows, so does the super-ego, incorporating values from school, church and society. However, it must be remembered that parents who first pass values on to the child also grew up in a society, and hence the parental standards are already socialized.

There is more to moral development, however, than merely knowing what the moral rules are, one must be motivated to act on them as well. The main reason that we act morally is fear of guilt. Guilt arises when internalization occurs. Sears, Rau and Alpert suggest that:

> According to Freud's theory the punitive-ness of the parents is converted by the child into self-punishment and the child learns to behave in ways suited to his parents' standards of conduct. Thus, the anticipation of punishment--originally from the parents, later from the self-- serves as the drive for developing resistence to the temptation to behave in ways antithetical to those standards.[85]

44

And Piers and Singer state:

> Both shame and guilt are highly important
> mechanisms to insure the socialization
> of the individual.

and

> Guilt transfers the demands of society
> through the early primitive parental
> images.[86]

On Freud's theory moral development in an individual
is measured in two ways: knowledge of the moral
values of one's group and the ability to comply
with those rules when tempted to break them.

The point, or function of morality on the
psychoanalytic view is to preserve social order,
social order being necessary to individual survival
and the survival of the species.[87] In <u>Civilization
and Its Discontents</u>, Freud makes it clear that we
need society to fulfill both physical and emotional
needs. Only a group is able to overcome the harsh,
unfriendly environment,[88] and only a group can
provide an outlet for our need for love.[89] In these
respects society is desirable.

Society also has its drawbacks. In order to
maintain social order, our sexual[90] and aggressive
instincts[91] must be kept in check. In order to
curb aggression, society induces people to turn
their aggression on themselves.[92] This is the
social function of the super-ego. The super-ego
redirects our aggressive tendencies towards
ourselves, in the form of guilt, for not living
up to our (internalized) standards. Freud says:
". . . the price of progress in civilization is
paid in forfeiting happiness through the heighten
ing of the sense of guilt."[93]

Morality, on this model, is a set of rules
designed to restrict otherwise desirable behavior.
The moral person is the one who acts in accordance

with these restrictions. The restrictions,
however, pose a dilemma: they are bound to cause
unhappiness (and often illness), yet they are
necessary for society, and we need society to
survive.

Interestingly, social-learning and behavioral
theories incorporate the same conception of morality as did Freud. Although they deny the presence
of a super-ego,[94] they nonetheless see morality as
a set of rules, and test for moral development by
looking at resistance to temptation and reaction
to transgression (guilt and shame).[95] Instead of
moral values being internalized through a process
of identification, moral rules are reinforced in
specific situations. If this reinforcement is
done correctly, the child will develop the moral
values in question. Being moral, once again, is
the ability to know and act on the moral values
of a group.

On either of these theories of morality and
moral acquisition, therapy presents an ideal
situation for adopting values in an uncritical way.
In fact, these theories virtually rule out the
possibility that moral values can be acquired in
a critical way. Critical reflection does not play
a rule in Freud's theory of identification and
internalization. According to Freud, the therapist
is likely to become an authority figure for the
client. If that client has developed a super-ego,
as all neurotics have, then the way is open for a
client to adopt the values he finds in therapy.

For social-learning and behavioral theorists,
therapy is a place where values can be reinforced
in a myriad of subtle ways. The quote from
Patterson in 1.3.2 was a behavioral explanation
of how clients learn values in therapy. Patterson
cited the "trace of a smile," "a pleased look" and
a "nod of the head" as ways in which a value can
be communicated and reinforced.

If values are present in therapy, as I have
argued they must be, both of these theories suggest

the strong possibility that a client will adopt
them uncritically. We can see, too, why the value-
free thesis would be an obvious solution to the
problem of dealing with client values: eliminating
values from therapy is the only way to insure that
these values will not be uncritically adopted by
the client. Hence, on both analytic and behavioral
theories, therapy is faced with a dilemma:
therapists will inevitably do what they must avoid.
This bodes ill for the client for two reasons:
first, he will unknowingly be inundated with a set
of values and second, this "inundation" is likely
to be anti-therapeutic. Therapy is ideally a
practice which encourages clients to work out
their problems for themselves. There are different
ways therapists try to do this, some more directive
than others, but no one, to my knowledge, thinks
that therapy is supposed to mold the client in a
specific way, and have the client approach and
solve problems just as the therapist would. Once
again we see that the problem of a client uncritically adopting values in therapy has ramifications for how therapy can be understood. Unless
some way can be given to avoid uncritical value
adoption, therapy as we normally conceive it is
impossible.

The dilemma described above, however, rests
on the view that moral development is fundamentally
a non-rational process. On the non-cognitive view
of morality and moral acquisition, reasons (qua
reasons) are not instrumental in the adoption of
moral values. If, however, it could be shown that
morality, or at least significant aspects of it,
not only could be but are rationally adopted
(which is not to say that they are reflectively
adopted) we would be forced to reevaluate the
effect of therapeutic and therapist values in
therapy. Whether or not rational considerations
do play an important role in moral development is
the subject of the next section.

2.3 Kohlberg's Cognitive-Developmental Approach to Morality

Recent work in cognitive moral development provides a solution to the dilemma which psycho-analytic and behavioral theories pose for therapy. The most complete theory of cognitive moral development is to be found in the work of Lawrence Kohlberg. Contrary to the theory that moral values are acquired through emotional identifica-tion or selective reinforcement, Kohlberg asserts that moral development is a result of the inter-action between a person's cognitive abilities and the structure of the social environment.[96] This is not to say that people simply adopt the moral codes of their society but rather that they understand their social environment in ways which determine both how they interpret moral codes and the importance of following those codes. Kohlberg has distinguished six stages of moral understanding through which people of various cultures progress. That this is a cross-cultural phenomenon is partly what prompts Kohlberg to reject analytic and[97] behavioral conceptions of moral development. If moral learning were simply a transmission of cultural values then cross-cultural regularity is not likely to occur. Further, as we shall see, there are cognitive limits to what can be internal-ized. This suggests that we cannot ignore cognitive processes in moral development even if the development involves non-cognitive elements as well.

In the exposition of Kohlberg's theory I will list the six stages of development. I will then discuss some general features of stage development, which will be followed by a discussion of the six stages. This latter discussion is designed to show how these general features are exemplified in actual cases of development. The six stages are:

I. Pre-conventional level

At this level the child is responsive to

48

cultural rules and labels of good and bad, right
or wrong, but interprets these labels in terms
of either the physical or the hedonistic consequences of action (punishment, reward, exchange
of favours) or in terms of the physical power of
those who enunciate the rules and labels. The
level comprises the following two stages:

Stage 1 punishment and obedience orientation

The physical consequences of action determine
its goodness or badness regardless of the
human meaning or value of these consequences.
Avoidance of punishment and unquestioning
deference to power are valued in their own
right, not in terms of respect for an under-
lying moral order supported by punishment
and authority (the latter being stage 4).

Stage 2 instrumental relativist orientation

Right action consists of that which instru-
mentally satisfies one's own needs and occa-
sionally the needs of others. Human relations
are viewed in terms similar to those of the
market place. Elements of fairness, of
reciprocity, and equal sharing are present,
but they are always interpreted in a physical
pragmatic way. Reciprocity is a matter of
"you scratch my back and I'll scratch yours,"
not of loyalty, gratitude, or justice.

II. Conventional level

At this level, maintaining the expectations of
the individual's family, group, or nation is perceived as valuable in its own right, regardless of
immediate and obvious consequences. The attitude
is one not only of conformity to personal expectations and social order, but of loyalty to it, of
actively maintaining, supporting, and justifying the
order, and of identifying with the persons or group
involved in it. This level comprises the following
two stages:

Stage 3   interpersonal concordance or "good
           boy-nice girl" orientation

Good behaviour is that which pleases or helps
others and is approved by them. There is
much conformity to stereotypical images of
what is majority or "natural" behaviour.
Behaviour is frequently judged by intention:
"he means well" becomes important for the
first time. One earns approval by being
"nice."

Stage 4   "law and order" orientation

There is orientation toward authority, fixed
rules, and the maintenance of the social
order. Right behaviour consists of doing
one's duty, showing respect for authority,
and maintaining the given social order for
its own sake.

III. Post-conventional, autonomous, or principled
      level

    At this level there is a clear effort to
define moral values and principles that have
validity and application apart from the authority
of the groups or persons holding these principles
and apart from the individual's own identification
with these groups. This level again has two stages:

Stage 5   social-contract legalistic orientation

Generally, this stage has utilitarian over-
tones. Right action tends to be defined in
terms of general individual rights and in
terms of standards that have been critically
examined and agreed upon by the whole society.
There is a clear awareness of the relativism
of personal values and opinions and a
corresponding emphasis on procedural rules
for reaching consensus. Aside from what is
constitutionally and democratically agreed

upon, the right is a matter of personal "values" and "opinion." The result is an emphasis upon the "legal point of view," but with an emphasis upon the possibility of changing law in terms of rational considerations of social utility, (rather than freezing it in terms of stage-4 "law and order"). Outside the legal realm, free agreement, and contract is the binding element of obligation. This is the "official" morality of the United States government and constitution.

Stage 6 <u>universal ethical-principle orientation</u>

Right is defined by the decision of conscience in accord with self-chosen <u>ethical principles</u> appealing to logical comprehensiveness, universality, and consistency. These principles are abstract and ethical (the Golden Rule, the categorical imperative); they are not concrete moral rules like the Ten Commandments. At heart, these are universal principles of justice, of the reciprocity and equality of human rights and of respect for the dignity of human beings as individual persons.[98]

In order to see the role of cognition in moral development it will be necessary to examine some general features of stage theory. The most basic of these features is the <u>structure-content</u> distinction. A stage, claims Kohlberg, is composed of beliefs which are related to one another in certain ways. Kohlberg refers to these beliefs as the <u>content</u> of the stage, and their relations to one <u>another</u> as the <u>structure</u> of a stage.[99] The feature that makes a stage unique is its structure, not its content. A simple example that illustrates this would be the case of two people both of whom believe that human life and

property ought to be preserved. If one person
valued life over property, and the other valued
property over life, they would have different
moral systems. This would be a case where the
same content yielded different personal morali-
ties. It is also possible that different content
could make up the same structure. Two girls could
abhor cheating, one because she will be spanked,
the other because she will not get dinner.
Although they offer different reasons for not
cheating they both have a hedonistic moral
structure.

Hierarchical integration is another important
aspect of stage theory. To say that a stage is a
hierarchical integration is to say that it
restructures the content (specific beliefs) of
the preceding stage.[100] Stage 2 restructures the
beliefs of stage 1, stage 3 restructures the
beliefs of stage 2, and so on. What this implies
is that each stage presupposes its antecedent
stage (this does not preclude new beliefs being
added at a later stage).

The fact that stages are hierarchically
integrated is part of the reason that the stages
form an invariant sequence. That is, the order
in which the stages are listed is the only order
in which people can pass through them.[101] To
reach stage 6, one must have reached stage 5; to
reach stage 5, one must have reached stage 4; etc.
The other factor supporting invariant sequence is
that the ability to comprehend the reasoning of
any stage is dependent on the ability to understand the previous stages. In this sense the
stages form a kind of cognitive hierarchy: one
simply cannot understand reasoning too far above
one's own.[102]

What we must consider next is the mechanism
of stage progression. Under what conditions is
a person motivated to adopt a new structure of
moral thought? To answer this we need to know
the function of a person's morality. Kohlberg

and Turiel posit two uses: to direct one's own behavior and to interpret the behavior of others.[103] Insofar as one's moral system cannot perform these functions, it will be inadequate and subject to change. On the subject of directing one's own behavior, a moral system can face two kinds of obstacles:

a) The presence of a moral problem which has aspects not covered by one's moral system.

b) The presence of a moral problem for which one's moral system prescribes incompatible solutions.

According to Kohlberg, problems such as a and b arise when one's moral system fails to differentiate relevant moral aspects, or if one's moral beliefs are not integrated to provide a single judgment. Since problems for a moral system arise from these factors, and since each stage is supposed to be more adequate than its predecessor, subsequent stages are claimed to be more differentiated and integrated.[104]

In order to see how these general features are exemplified, I will discuss the six stages in more detail. But before doing that I need to mention briefly how Kohlberg gets his data, since I will quote from interviews conducted by Kohlberg and his colleagues. The primary tool used to collect data is the moral judgment questionnaire. The questionnaire consists of a story describing a moral dilemma followed by a list of questions about that dilemma. The following is one of the more popular questionnaires used by Kohlberg:

> In Europe a woman was near death from a special kind of cancer. There was one drug that the doctors thought might save her. It was a form of radium that a druggist in the same town had recently discovered. The drug was expensive to make, but the druggist was charging ten

times the amount the drug had cost him
to make. He paid $200 for the radium
and charged $2000 for a small dose of
the drug. The sick woman's husband,
Heinz, went to everyone he knew to borrow
the money, but he could only get together
about $1000 which is half of what it cost.
He told the druggist that his wife was
dying and asked him to sell it cheaper
or let him pay later. The druggist said,
"No, I discovered the drug and I'm
going to make money from it." So Heinz
got desperate, and broke into the man's
store to steal the drug for his wife.

Should Heinz steal the drug? Why? Which
is worse, letting someone die or stealing?
What does the value of life mean to you?
Is there good reason for a husband to
steal if he doesn't love his wife? Would
it be right to steal for a stranger as
to steal for his wife? If Heinz is
caught and brought to trial, should the
judge sentence him? Why? What is the
responsibility of the judge to society in
this case?[105]

Not all of these questions would be asked of
everyone. The point of having this list is to
provide a list of questions which can be used to
bring out the moral reasoning being used.

One problem which this kind of moral research
must overcome is the tendency of a subject to try
to please the experimenter, or to give "accepted"
answers. For example, very few people would say
that shoplifting or lying is morally acceptable,
even if they thought it was. Kohlberg's tests
overcome this difficulty in two ways: first,
the kinds of problems he gives often do not have
"accepted" solutions; second, and more important-
ly, Kohlberg's primary aim is not to find out if
a subject believes that a particular act is right
or wrong. Kohlberg is more interested in how

the subject justifies moral judgments. Although
a subject may fake specific responses, it is
unlikely that he would be able to misrepresent
the way he reasons about moral problems. There
are two reasons why it is unlikely that a subject
would "fake" reasoning. First, people usually
believe that the reasoning which is below their
level is inadequate;[106] it is unlikely that they
would find reasoning associated with stages lower
than their own as "accepted" or as reasoning that
would please the experimenter. Second, the subject
is not likely to fake reasoning higher than his
own, since there is evidence that suggests that
this is impossible. Subjects cannot usually
understand stages more than one level above their
own.[107] Hence, there is good reason to think that
the reasoning exhibited by subjects is the
reasoning they actually employ.

We are almost ready to examine the six basic
types of moral reasoning. Before we do, two
warnings are in order. The first is that I will
use "ideal" examples of stage progression.
Although stage 3 reasoning, for example, could
conceivably be employed within peer groups, or in
orphanges, I will speak of stage 3 as a family
oriented stage. Similarly, although stage 4
reasoning could be used to justify behavior to
support religious sects, racial dominance or
cultural integrity, I will describe stage 4 as
identifying with a nation. My aim is to explain
how stage development progresses. Once I have
done this the reader will be able to see how and
why some people might diverge from the usual
developmental path.

The second is that Kohlberg is investigating
moral judgment, not moral behavior. When I
describe a stage 3 view that physical punishment
should be avoided because "good children do not
get punished," one may think that this is
unrealistic. The reason that children avoid such
punishment is because it hurts. Of course, when
it comes to acting in the face of punishment, it

may very well be that pain of punishment will deter a child. This does not imply, however, that the child judges that the act is wrong because of the punishment. It only shows that he may be motivated by fear to act in accordance with what he judges to be the right course of action.

Kohlberg says that stage 1 "defines the 'socio-moral order' in terms of differentials of power, status and possessions. . . . The 'principles' maintaining social order are obedience to the strong by the weak and punishment by the strong of those who deviate."[108] What is judged as "wrong" is that for which one is punished. A typical stage 1 reason for not lying or not breaking a promise is that one will be punished for these acts. Hence, if punishment can be avoided stage 1 reasoning could support lying or promise breaking. In response to the Heinz example two stage 1 individuals said:

Pro: If you let your wife die, you will get into trouble.

Con: You shouldn't steal the drug because you'll be caught and sent to jail if you do.[109]

Stage 1 is characterized by limited role-taking and the inability to go beyond immediate consequences in making moral judgments. For example, the interests of the dying wife, or the effect of her death on the rest of the family are not mentioned.

Stage 1 will be inadequate for many reasons. As the child grows, he is likely to see others keep their promises or tell the truth (when it would be more advantageous to deceive) even though there is no expected punishment. Further, the child might come to realize that deceitful behavior can have other kinds of consequences than a single bout of punishment, such as others ceasing to believe him.

Stage 1's inability to explain the action of others, and its unsatisfactory direction of one's own behavior is what motivates a change to stage 2. Kohlberg characterizes this stage as one of instrumental relativism. In contrast to stage 1, which perceives society as merely a limiting force, stage 2 sees social organization as an instrument which can be used to promote one's own interest. The stage 2 justification for not lying or promise breaking, for example, might rest on the fact that people will not trust a liar. With respect to the Heinz example, stage 2 children from Taiwan (the story was changed to fit their culture) thought that Heinz should steal the drug because funerals are very expensive.[110] In an Atayal village stage 2 children advocated stealing the drug because a wife is useful; she will clean and cook.[111] Stage 2 reasoning could also advocate not stealing the drug: the risk is great and one could always remarry.

Stage 2 is an advance over stage 1 in many ways. The practice of truth telling and the institution of promising are better understood. In stage 1 the injunction against lying was viewed much as an obscure rule of etiquette: just another arbitrary rule. In stage 2, however, the child begins to understand how these practices and institutions work, how they can structure the social environment. Along with this comes an advance in understanding reciprocal relationships and role-taking. One way that a child comes to know that lying breeds distrust is that he is able to take the role of another, and can see that reciprocal relationships depend on participants being honest. What characterizes stage 2, though, is not that the child acts, or even judges in favor of supporting useful institutions or reciprocal relationships. The advance of stage 2 is the ability to understand why these are important considerations and to be able to integrate these considerations in deliberation. For example, if we added to the Heinz example that stealing was punishable by horrible torture, most stage 2 responses would not advocate stealing the drug because the torture outweighs the usefulness of a wife. Still a stage 2 individual could understand why both of these considerations are important in a way a stage 1 respondent could not.

Stage 2 runs into problems when it is unable to explain the actions of others. Parents, for example, may do things which they openly dislike and for which the child can see no immediate or long term benefit. Coupled with this is a growing perception of the family as a group to which one is tied in special ways. The understanding of reciprocal relationships which formed the basis of stage 2 gives the child the conceptual equipment to understand the family as a group and to realize how different roles contribute to the welfare of that group.

The child's increased understanding of the social environment is partly what prompts a stage 3 appeal to the family as a moral authority, with the parents as representatives of this authority. Lying and promise breaking are wrong because good children do not act in these ways. That is, the role of a good child is incompatible with lying and cheating. Punishment is still important, but only as a result of wrongdoing. It is no longer the punishment that makes the act wrong, rather, family expectations are invoked to show that an act is wrong. In response to the Heinz example stage 3 individuals advocate stealing the drug because only an "inhuman husband" would not steal it.[112] Stage 3 reasoning to support not stealing the drug sometimes cites the dishonor that would be brought upon the family.[113]

Stage 3 is an advance over 2 in that the child is able to differentiate the interests of the group from its members. Stage 2's limited understanding of group life prevented this. The child begins to identify his interests with family interests, not because he is being inundated with the importance of family life but because he sees himself as a member of this group to which all contribute. Role-taking is expanded in that a child begins to consider the interests of others in themselves instead of in terms of what others can do for him. This advance in role-taking is also shown in the ability to weigh good intentions. Bad acts can sometimes be forgiven if the agent meant well.[114]

Stage 3, though, still has certain problems. First, it does not account for non-familial obligations. A family oriented morality will not work well in school, for example, nor will it explain the power that governmental agencies have. Hence, it does not fully comprehend the social structure, and will be inadequate to direct behavior in many situations. If a child is made to clean up after himself in school, but not at home, relying on family rules would obviously be troublesome. In the face of conflicting rules and the inability to explain the social environment, the child is very likely to emerge into stage 4.

In stage 4 a person appeals to the authority of the state or the community to determine moral worth. Lying and promise breaking are wrong because the community forbids that type of behavior. Acting in those ways would destroy the community and should be forbidden. In response to the Heinz example, a typical stage 4 response would be that Heinz was wrong to steal the drug, because stealing is against the law. Stage 4 could be used to support Heinz as well. If it was thought that community standards put family loyalty above property laws in this kind of case, Heinz's act could be justified.

Stage 4's immediate advancement over 3 is the ability to differentiate between familial obligations and obligations we have in virtue of being citizens and members of other groups.

59

A person needs some way to sort out these obligations, and stage 3 is clearly inadequate to do this. Further, stage 4 represents a better understanding of the social environment. In complex societies group life is regulated and determined by all sorts of factors which interact in complicated ways. Stage 4 represents the ability to deal with these factors better than stage 3. Significant role-taking is expanded to members outside the family. Stage 4, for example, is the first stage in which the druggist (in the Heinz example) is morally considered.

Stage 4, although a significant advance over 3, will still have problems. A major problem will be in justifying laws and practices which are challenged. Since stage 4 justifies laws on the grounds that they exist, or that they maintain order, how can it understand the charge that laws can be immoral even though they maintain order? This is linked to the problem of legislation. What criteria should be used in making laws?[115] Stage 4 is not adequate in these respects. Further, there is the problem of moral obligations to those outside the state,[116] and the need to adjudicate international conflicts. These are all issues of which most are aware, and for which stage 4 provides unsatisfactory answers.

These are the kind of problems that lead to stage 5, which attempts to explain moral obligations in terms of a social contract or utility. For example, lying and promise breaking are wrong because truth-telling and promising are practices to which we all could agree, or that are extremely utile. Their utility, though, is not merely measured by how they maintain the group, but rather how they serve the interests of all the members of the group. "Law and order" is still important, but only because it protects individuals or is that to which all individuals agree. In response to the Heinz example, stage 5 reasoning could support stealing the drug on the grounds that property laws, which are designed to protect and preserve life, are not serving their original purpose. Hence, in this kind of case theft is justified. Stage 5 reasoning rejecting the theft could admit that a life is very important, but that the theft put other members of society in jeopardy.

Once again, we can see that role-taking has expanded. This is the first stage in which the life of the dying woman is taken as morally important in itself. This represents the ability to identify with the woman, i.e., take her role apart from her relation to a group. This stage has a way to justify laws, and hence clarifies the role of the legislator. Moral obligations to those outside the state, and adjudicating international conflicts can be understood since stage 5 morality is not relative to a specific group.

According to Kohlberg, stage 5 has two major problems: it is unable to appreciate the necessity of civil disobedience[117] and it cannot solve conflicts between welfare and justice (whether these are legitimate problems will be discussed in 2.3.2). Kohlberg views civil disobedience as clearly justifiable in some instances, hence any theory that cannot account for it is deficient. The other problem is the conflict between justice and welfare.[118] Kohlberg asserts that stage 5 is incapable of deliberating about this conflict because it has not clearly differentiated welfare concerns from justice.

These problems are solved by stage 6 which determines morality by an appeal to conscience, employing the criteria of consistency, universality and justice. Lying and promise breaking are wrong because one could not universalize these acts and further, these acts would violate the rights of those who are deceived. The Heinz dilemma would be solved by an appeal to conscience and the principles of justice. Consider the

61

following stage 6 response to the Heinz dilemma
given by an anonymous philosopher:

> [Heinz] was wrong legally, but right
> morally. I believe that one has at
> least a _prima facie_ duty to save a life
> (when he is in a position to do so) and
> in this case, the legal duty not to
> steal is clearly outweighed by the moral
> duty to save a life.

and

> In the case of conflict between the
> imperative of a specific law and a moral
> imperative, one can often "see" or
> intuit that one "ought" to break a law
> in order to fulfill a moral duty.[119]

As we have described stage development, it
progresses because a stage faces certain kinds
of problems. Those problems forced the reasoner
to evaluate the situation differently, differen-
tiating various moral considerations and
integrating them in a way that will yield a
single judgment. One might object that stage 6
can encounter problems as well: if two persons
lives were in danger and were equally deserving
and a stage 6 individual could only save one of
them, which one should he choose? Do such
dilemmas imply that existence of a stage 7? Not
necessarily. Kohlberg could argue that moral
life is so complex that it will present problems
for any moral system. The best moral system,
then, is not the one that presents clear solutions
to all moral problems but the one that enables
us to understand the different moral considerations that apply. This increase in understanding
is the major reason Kohlberg believes in the
moral superiority of stage 6.

2.3.1 Comparison of Kohlberg's Theory of Moral Development with the Competing Non-Cognitive View

A cognitive-developmental theory is superior to a strict internalization or reinforcement theory: it explains all the phenomena which the non-cognitive theories explain, whereas the non-cognitive theories cannot adequately explain the data on which cognitive theory is based. A basic fact for which any theory of moral development must account is the continuity of values across generations. A natural way to explain this is that children simply copy the values they find in society. The question, then, is what is the mechanism involved in this learning process? Freud postulated the development of a super-ego which uncritically adopts the values found in the environment. Freud's theory was fraught with problems, one of which was the difficulty of designing experiments to test this theory. Problems with the analytic approach led to the growth of behavioral and social learning views. They agreed with Freud that values were uncritically acquired but postulated a different mechanism of adoption: reinforcement replaced emotional identification. Both Freud's and the behaviorist's model of moral development are adequate to explain moral continuity.

These theories, however, have trouble explaining the fact that moral development progresses in an orderly fashion, and that people of different cultures follow similar developmental patterns. They also fail to account for the difference in how individuals understand rules they find in society. Consider the injunction against lying. In one sense, persons in stages 1-6 may know and follow this rule. Kohlberg, however, has given us good reason to think that the adoption of this rule in various stages is only superficially similar. A stage 1 individual, for example, thinks lying is wrong only because one will be punished, whereas a stage 5 individual would reject lying on the grounds that it violates the rights of persons or is a practice which is not utile. Kohlberg has shown that in assessing a person's morality we need to know more than that a set of rules has been adopted. We need to know how a person understands and justifies these rules. In the jargon of cognitive-developmental theory, a person's morality is not merely a function of content, but of how that content is structured. It is this notion of structure, or how a person understands the values with which he is confronted, which non-cognitive theories cannot explain. Given the importance of this aspect of a person's morality, strict non-cognitivist theories of moral development must fail.

On the cognitive model of moral development, cultural values are adopted by future generations because they make sense: they help persons understand and direct their behavior within their environment. If a person's moral training does not yield an adequate understanding of the social environment, if it does not work to guide behavior, it will very likely be rejected. For example, on Kohlberg's theory, a child who believes his parents are cruel, insensitive people is less likely to adopt a stage 3 type of reasoning than a child with a more stable family environment.

Moral content then, is cognitively mediated. That is, how we understand the rules and injunctions of society is tempered by how we interpret our social environment and our place in it. How we understand our social environment is reflected by our moral structure. Since one's structure is a function of one's understanding, and since understanding is not the kind of thing that can be drilled in or inculcated, it follows that a significant part of a person's moral system cannot arise from direct social influence. Of course, we can coerce someone to spend time on some subject, and hope that he will come to understand it. This is not inculcating

understanding, though. It is creating an environment in which we hope the person will come to
understand.

It is also important to note that Kohlberg's
psychological analysis of a moral system (i.e.,
a stage) more closely approximates the philosophical model of a moral system than the competing
non-cognitive theories. Moral theorists (e.g.,
Ross, Rawls) recognize the importance of a system
of priority for moral values. Such a priority
system is necessary since conflict between moral
values is a significant and common kind of moral
problem. When such a problem arises, an agent
must employ or generate some set of priorities.
In Kohlberg's theory the priority system is
reflected in one's structure. Non-cognitive
theories can account for priority only in non-
rational terms, such as strength of identification or reinforcement. Kohlberg's findings,
however, would tend to refute this account of
the development of a priority system. Since
priorities are a function of structure, and since
the development of structure is not tied to any
particular environmental influence, it would
appear that an individual system of priorities
could not be explained in terms of identification
or reinforcement.

In light of Kohlberg's theory, our problem
as described in 2.1 is somewhat lessened. Direct
influence is limited, and so is the ability of
the therapist to influence the client's moral
values. Still, stages 3 and 4, in that they
appeal to authority, pose a problem. Persons
in these stages are very likely to adopt values
that the appropriate authority figures support.
Since the therapist is often viewed by the client
as an authority, stages 3 and 4 are open to what
amounts to an uncritical adoption of values. It
is uncritical in the sense that values will not
be evaluated in terms of their usefulness or
appropriateness, but in terms of authority
approval. As I mentioned, this haphazard method

of value adoption is not likely to lead to a salutary set of values. In more normal circumstances, a person is able to sort out the inconsistent or vague moral values he adopts in these stages; it is this process of sorting out one's values that leads to stage progression. In fact, one person has suggested that therapeutic clients do not have more value conflicts than others, but that they have more difficulty in resolving them.[120] If so, this underscores the anti-therapeutic nature of uncritical value adoption. If clients generally have a hard time integrating their values, adding more values in therapy can be especially dangerous.

This does not contradict Kohlberg's conception of moral development as a cognitive process, since he was concerned with development, and not primarily with acquisition of beliefs within a stage. It is true that what one learns in any given stage will be mediated by the structure of that stage; but we can assume that stage 3 and 4 individuals, the ones which cause the most concern, will be sophisticated enough to have a fairly good understanding of the values expressed by the therapist.

The way to solve the problem that stage 3 and 4 individuals pose for therapy is to help clients adopt a stage 5 or 6 type of reasoning. Kohlberg and Turiel have suggested fairly effective ways to do this. If this could be achieved, a client who uncritically adopts moral values in therapy would eventually be in a position to evaluate the values adopted earlier. This program, however, has its own problem. Is it morally justifiable to structure therapy in a way that is designed to change the client's moral point of view? Even if the amount of direct influence that a therapist can exert is limited, he is still taking an active role in changing the moral understanding of the client. What about the moral system that results from such a program? Is it morally justifiable? Would it be possible to characterize a therapist's attempt to alter the cognitive elements of a client's moral system as indoctrinative? Kohlberg argues that promoting stage development is not indoctrinative, and that any given stage of moral development is morally superior to all preceding stages. I will evaluate these claims in the next section.

2.3.2 Kohlberg's Ethical Justification of Stage Development

Kohlberg offers a three-fold justification to show that promoting stage development is not indoctrinative:

1) Stage progression is not the result of any direct influence, but is a consequence of attempting to understand the social environment.[121]

2) A stage does not determine which course of action will be taken in response to a problem.[122]

3) Higher stages are morally superior to lower ones.[123]

I will examine these in order.

Although I do not dispute the truth of #1, it does not show that promoting stage development is not indoctrinative. If it were true that particular stages were associated with particular judgments and ways of reacting towards problems, the following situation could arise: A person who wishes to indoctrinate a set of beliefs realizes that one stage is much more likely to adopt those beliefs than another. Consequently, he uses cognitive educational methods to advance students to that stage with the goal of getting them to adopt those specific beliefs. Clearly, the fact the students progressed to the higher stages because of their tendency to restructure their beliefs into a more differentiated and

67

integrated form (see 2.3) does not show that indoctrination cannot take place. An effective indoctrinator would use a person's cognitive abilities to encourage certain beliefs. The most amenable stages for inculcation would be stage 3 or 4, both of which appeal to a socially backed standard of authority.

Kohlberg, however, argues that a stage does not completely determine how specific moral problems will be resolved. This claim has its theoretical basis in the structure-content distinction. In order to reliably predict how a person will resolve a particular moral issue, we need to know both the structure and the content of his moral reasoning. The hedonist presents a clear example: although we know that the hedonist will try to maximize pleasure, in order to predict his judgments reliably we will need to know what he finds pleasurable. Similarly, persons in stages 3-4 determine moral worth by an appeal to authority, but unless we know what constitutes the authority (church leaders, national leaders, peer groups) we will not be able to predict specific responses. Finally, in Level III, where one begins to develop one's own moral code, there is little chance of predicting how specific problems will be resolved. In 2.3 I tried to show how a stage could be used to support incompatible solutions to a dilemma.

Moral education concentrates on the structure of a person's reasoning, not the content. Classes in moral education do not emphasize any particular moral view. Rather, students are encouraged to discuss how they reason about moral problems. The moral educator acts as a catalyst to discussion, trying to indicate inconsistencies or lines of reasoning that students develop. Since no particular view is emphasized, it is hard to see how a moral educator or a therapist employing this method could be accused of indoctrination.

One problem with this justification is the fact that to criticize a moral view is to voice a moral opinion. For example, to claim that two judgments are inconsistent is to suppose that there are no morally significant differences that justify the divergent judgments. Suppose a person claimed that it is justifiable to tell a lie to his parents, but that it would be wrong to tell that same lie to his friends. It may be that this person thinks that there are morally relevant differences in these situations. Hence, to say that those two judgments are inconsistent is to express a moral view about relevant differences.

Another problem is the ability of a person to adopt a value even though it may not be stressed (see 1.3.2). Further, there is always the possibility that a value may be stressed even though there is an attempt not to stress the value (see 1.3.2). It is clear that content must be discussed in a class designed to advance moral reasoning, since moral reasoning is reasoning about content. For therapy, then, Kohlberg's second justification does not hold.

Still, we could argue that in spite of the danger of acquiring specific beliefs, relying on Kohlberg's techniques is the best way to discuss values in therapy. No solution will be perfect, but at least his system prescribes the most effective method of preventing clients from uncritically adopting values in therapy.

There is, however, the following difficulty. Kohlberg's argument so far has depended on the assumption that stages can be used to support either side of an action choice. Although this is true, it is not strong enough. Kohlberg needs to show that a stage is <u>neutral</u> with respect to action choices. That is, even though a stage could be used to support incompatible solutions to a problem, isn't it possible that stages, in fact, tend to support certain kinds of judgments? For example, since stage 4 is the "law and order" stage, is it not likely that the interests of the community as expressed in its legal system would take priority?

This assumption is borne out by two independent studies. Haan, Smith and Block examined participators and non-participators in campus demonstrations in Berkeley. The university was restricting the release of information which some student groups thought should be open to the public. The researchers found that stage 6 individuals were eight times more likely to sit-in than those in stages 3 or 4.[124] In a study conducted by Milgram, where subjects were intimidated to inflict pain on another person, 75% of stage 6 individuals refused, whereas only 13% of the lower stages did so.[125] What such studies reveal is obvious: to be in a stage is to have a strong tendency to act in certain ways. This shows that the process of encouraging stage development can result in specific tendencies even though those tendencies are not supported or reinforced by the therapist. Kohlberg's second argument to justify encouraging stage development fails. If, however, Kohlberg successfully argues that a stage of moral development is morally superior to its antecedent stages, creating an environment conducive to that development would seem to be justified. Although stage development would affect the way one acts in situations, the change would be for the better.

Kohlberg has two arguments to show the moral superiority of later stages. The first argument relies on a formalist ethical theory and the other invokes a concept of justice. I will discuss these arguments in order.

Briefly, ethical formalism is the view that a judgment is moral if and only if the agent is ready to prescribe that all persons in similar situations should act in accordance with that judgment. On this view, a defensible moral judgment is one that is prescriptive and which the agent is ready to universalize. Kohlberg presents an argument which attempts to correlate differentiation with prescriptivity and integration with universality.[126] Kohlberg claims that as moral stages become differentiated and integrated they become more prescriptive and more universal.[127] It can be conclusively shown that this correlation does not succeed.[128] However, even though this correlation fails, it could still be true that a person in a later stage is more likely to universalize his prescriptive judgments than a person in an earlier stage. Hence, the important consideration here is the adequacy of formalism, not Kohlberg's claim that differentiation and integration map onto prescriptivity and universality.

Before we test for the adequacy of formalism, it will be useful to ask what the appeal is of a theory of ethics whose only criterion of a moral judgment is the ability of the agent to universalize a prescriptive judgment. There are at least two considerations that recommend it. One is that people can make very different moral judgments, employ very different moral criteria, without any of them being immoral. Formalism, by ignoring content, gives us a way to understand moral diversity without being forced to judge some of these moral positions as immoral or indefensible. Another reason why formalism may be appealing is that it would "work" for most people. I would think that a person of normal intelligence and sympathies who was asked to guide his moral life by formal criteria would very likely make moral judgments with which most would agree.

Even though formalism is appealing in the above ways, there are serious problems with it. Although most people's self-interest or sympathy would keep them from universalizing judgments which prescribe genocide, it is possible for a person to universalize such a judgment.

71

Consider a Nazi, who prescribes the extermina-
tion of Jews. The requirement of universalizability requires that he put himself and his
family to death _if_ he discovers that he and his
wife are Jewish. If the Nazi is willing to
accept this and all the other consequences of
Nazism then that Nazi holds moral views against
which no cogent moral arguments could be made.
Clearly, however, the Nazi prescription for
genocide is not only not moral, it is immoral.

The suggestion that the last stages of moral
development yield universal prescriptive judgments will not show that these stages are morally
superior. Any non-self-contradictory prescription can be universalized if the agent is willing
to subject himself to the treatment prescribed.
What is often important is what the judgment
prescribes, not the form of the prescription.

Kohlberg's other justification for promoting
moral development is that it accords with the
principle of justice. Kohlberg's most compre-
hensive statement on the nature of justice is
the following:

> We take the word "justice" to mean a
> moral resolution of competing claims,
> that is, a reference to a method of
> distributing or defining claims. The
> basic rule of justice is distributive
> equality: treat every man equally. We
> recognize, however, that people also have
> special claims on the individual moral
> actor or upon the state. These claims
> are based on commutative justice or
> reciprocity, and include keeping con-
> tracts or trusts, undoing harm done,
> and showing gratitude as some return
> for service and effort. While there is
> no single accepted principle of
> justice which orders all these aspects,
> we generally assume a sphere of human
> rights in which equality takes priority

over the special claims of commutative justice.[129]

It is the priority of distributive justice over commutative justice that represents an advance over stage 5. This priority is the justification of civil disobedience. Kohlberg says:

> The core problem which stage 5 cannot resolve is the problem of the conditions under which it is morally right or obligatory to violate the law. The principles of welfare and social contract are inadequate to resolve this problem.[130]

That is, stage 6 can see that distributive equality is morally prior to obeying laws; hence, when they conflict only a stage 6 individual is able to invoke the distributive principle as a justification for disobeying the law.

In my discussion of Kohlberg's theory of justice I will concentrate on two things: a) is it true that a stage 5 conception of moral duty cannot account for civil disobedience and, apart from that, b) is a stage 6 conception of justice viable on moral grounds? Before doing that, I want to explain why I am not going to discuss stages 1-4 in terms of justice. It does not seem that any of those stages is more just or is more likely to produce just solutions to moral problems than any other stage. Whether any stage among the first 4 would be more just would depend on non-stage factors. For stages 1 and 2, one would opt for the just solution if that solution is judged to be better on hedonistic grounds. Hence, in an environment where it is to one's interest to be just one would be just. Epicurus, for example, argued that it was in one's interest to be just in a well-ordered society.[131] Stages 3 and 4, since they base their judgments on an appeal to authority, will choose the just solution to moral dilemmas insofar as the authority to which they appeal is just. We know, of course, that the justness of an act will never be a reason for making a particular judgment in stages 1-4, but that says nothing about the justness of the solution. Although there is no way to show that any one of the first 4 stages is more just than another, promoting stage progression through the early stages can be justified by the moral superiority of stages 5 and 6, since advancing through stages 1-4 is the only way to reach the last two stages.

With stages 1-4 set aside, I will begin discussing Kohlberg's justification of the last stage of moral development. Is stage 6, as Kohlberg claims, the only stage in which civil disobedience can be justified? If we look at stage 5, which relies on utilitarian and con- tractual ethical theories, we can see how civil disobedience can be justified without stage 6 reasoning. For an act utilitarian, there is no problem in justifying civil disobedience. Since each act is judged by the utility of its consequences, any act of disobeying the law that is more utile than acting in accordance with the law would be morally acceptable, and perhaps obligatory. Although Kohlberg does not talk about act utilitarianism, it is clear that it is a stage 5 type of reasoning. It is based upon the welfare of all, and is not tied to any particular group. Hence, it cannot be a part of stage 1-4 reasoning. Act utilitarianism cannot be a part of stage 6, since it does not differentiate justice from utility in the appropriate way. For an act utilitarian, such as Smart, justice is moral only insofar as it maximizes utility, and when utility and justice conflict, utility should be the overriding consideration.[132]

Even a rule utilitarian could argue for civil disobedience in some cases. If a law is clearly immoral (non-utile) and if civil

74

disobedience is the only way to motivate a society to change the law, then civil disobedience could be justified. Of course one of the mainstays of rule utilitarianism is the utility of _rules_, and the insistence that that utility results from the general observance of these rules. Civil disobedience would be justified, then, when the utility of that disobedience and its effects on the society was more utile than not being disobedient.[133] Although a rule utilitarian would allow much fewer acts of civil disobedience than an act utilitarian (in our world, at least), it is a mistake to think that a rule utilitarian could not consistently prescribe civil disobedience.

It is also easy to see how civil disobedience could be justified by contract theory. Contract theory does not prescribe that all laws should be kept at all times simply because the populus has agreed to those laws. Laws are justified insofar as all people could rationally agree to them, leaving all personal interest aside. What counts as "rational agreement" and how to insure that personal interests are not involved are problems contract theorists must solve. However, it is clear that if a law is so bad that rational agreement is impossible, then civil disobedience might be necessary. Of course, the injustice of a law does not, in itself, justify civil disobedience. Rawls, in "The Justification of Civil Disobedience," offers a detailed explanation of how civil disobedience could be justified within a social contract theory. For example, Rawls stipulates that civil disobedience is justified only as a last resort and only if the persons engaging in the disobedience are willing to universalize their actions in those circumstances.[134] Once again a social contract theorist is less likely to prescribe civil disobedience than an act utilitarian, but that does not imply that civil disobedience would never be justified on contractual grounds.

This argument for preferring stage 6 over 5 fails. Still, it could be that stage 6 is preferable for other reasons. I now will argue that it is not.

The main problem with stage 6 is what Kohlberg hails as its major virtue: the ability to distinguish commutative from distributive justice and the tendency to judge that the latter is prior to the former. One problem with stage 6 is its vagueness: Kohlberg admits that there is no single principle by which the special claims of commutative justice can be ordered, but in general equality should be prior to any special claim.[135] The preferred moral system, then, is one which is essentially unpredictable. For example, if one makes a promise with a stage 6 individual, one should expect that promise to be kept only if it does not conflict with distributive equality. Moral philosophers as divergent as Kant and Hume have seen the folly of this reasoning. If promises will be kept only insofar as they do not conflict with distributive equality, the institution of promising would be severely weakened. It must be remembered that the keeping of a promise would depend on how the promisor evaluates the act of keeping the promise. If he judges that keeping the promise does not promote distributive equality he will be obligated to break the promise.

Although there may be cases where distributive concerns override commutative concerns, to make this a general principle is going too far. Society could not survive if it allowed and taught individuals that each instance of following a law should be a matter of conscience; are we supposed to decide whether following a law at a time conflicts with distributive equality? How could we do this? A major benefit of having rules and laws is to eliminate personal judgment to a degree, so as to insure an order in which personal judgment, in other

76

areas of one's life, can be effective. If I
decide to do something, but cannot count on
others to do what they regularly do, or what
they say they will do, then I cannot reasonably
expect to fulfill my plans.

I want to make clear that I am arguing
against stage 6 insofar as it is a mode of
ordinary practical reason. It may very well be
that a person qua legislator should take a
stage 6 perspective. A legislator should at
least be beyond stage 4. The major principle
guiding a stage 4 legislator would be the
effectiveness of a law in supporting the existing conventions of a society. But what if
these conventions conflict? Or what if problems
arise for which there are no accepted solutions,
such as euthanasia? There is the stage 4
principle of efficiency: adopt legislation
which best promotes law and order. Such a
principle, however, is likely to be inadequate
to solve problems such as euthanasia. Although
considerations of efficiency are appropriate in
making any law, there are often other factors,
moral factors, which should be considered. For
example, a stage 4 legislator may vote in favor
of a liberal euthanasia bill in order to ease
hospital bed shortages. Conspicuously absent
from such reasoning is an interest in those
who will die as a result of this legislation.
Surely they need to be considered as well.
There is good reason to think, then, that
stage 4 would be inadequate to guide legislation. Apart from this, however, a stage 4
acceptance of the laws of society (excluding
extraordinary circumstances) may be the best moral
path even if those laws are not the best laws
that could be enacted. This is only to suggest
that there is a difference between rule-making
and rule-following that can have moral ramifications. An adequate moral justification for
voting against a law is not always an adequate
justification for breaking that law.

The argument above relies on the distinction between justifying a practice and justifying an act that falls under that practice. Although there may be good reason to reject or alter an existing practice, that does not imply that there are good reasons to violate that practice. No doubt there can be reasons for violating practices. My point is that stage 6 reasoning, if it is justifiable at all, speaks mainly to practices, not to acts falling under practices.

The same argument applies to stage 5. Although its principles may be the best way to organize a society, this does not speak to its workability as a system of everyday practical moral reasoning. Kohlberg, however, attempts to promote stages 5 and 6 as ways in which all moral problems should be solved. He makes this clear in his defense of the "generality" thesis, one of the more intensely debated aspects of Kohlberg's theory. According to Kohlberg, to be in a moral stage is to have a "total way of thinking," that is, a person tends to interpret all situations in terms of his stage.[136] To promote stages 5 or 6, then, is to promote that kind of reasoning in all situations. I have tried to show that there are ethical considerations which speak against this kind of generality.

Promoting stages 5 and 6, then, could be morally disastrous, especially if the generality thesis is correct. Kohlberg is arguing for the later stages on the grounds that they provide better solutions to all problems. This, however, is not something we can know in advance. There may be kinds of situations in which stages 5 or 6 would not be the best mode of practical reasoning.

2.4 Conclusion

My major goal in this chapter has been to clarify the problem of clients adopting moral values in therapy and to show how that problem could be solved. I have argued that the specific problem on which I am concentrating is not indoctrination, but is one that closely resembles it, viz., a client's propensity to adopt values in therapy in an uncritical way. I then suggested that we could not properly assess value adoption in therapy apart from an understanding of how people develop morally. I showed that a non-cognitive view of moral development (on which both psychoanalysts and behaviorists rely) makes the problem of uncritical value adoption in therapy insoluble since value adoption is explained solely in terms of uncritical processes. A cognitive view of moral development (which I argued is superior to the non-cognitive view) shows that moral values can be adopted in a critical way. This theory shows that a solution to our problem is possible if we can justify promoting the moral development of the client. Kohlberg's justifications for promoting moral development are inadequate. Hence, the cognitive theory of moral development has difficulties which prevent it from being used to discuss moral values in therapy.

In the next chapter I will try to show that the ethical objections to cognitive developmental programs of moral education described above are not to the point. I will argue that Kohlberg's approach to the problem of indoctrination is misguided, primarily because he fails to distin-guish moral influence from moral indoctrination. The failure to recognize this difference has prevented him from realizing that there can be cases of direct, specific moral influence which are not indoctrinative.

[67] I borrow much of this discussion from I. A. Snook, Indoctrination and Education.

[68] I. A. Snook, Indoctrination and Education, p. 38.

[69] Ibid., p. 41.

[70] Ibid.

[71] Ibid., p. 27.

[72] Ibid., p. 29.

[73] Ibid., p. 37.

[74] Ibid., p. 22.

[75] Ibid., p. 47.

[76] For more on how therapy can be viewed as an educational process, see Thomas Szasz, The Ethics of Psychoanalysis.

[77] See Sigmund Freud, The Ego and the Id.

[78] Sigmund Freud, The Ego and the Id, p. 30.

[79] Ibid., p. 28.

[80] Ibid., p. 39.

[81] Ibid., p. 46.

[82] Ibid.

[83] Ibid., p. 69.

[84] Sigmund Freud, On Narcissism, p. 96.

[85] Robert Sears, Lucy Rau and Richard Alpert, _Identification and Child Rearing_, p. 199.

[86] Gerhart Piers and Milton Singer, _Shame and Guilt_, p. 53.

[87] Sigmund Freud, _Civilization and Its Discontents_, p. 95.

[88] Ibid., p. 77.

[89] Ibid., pp. 82, 101.

[90] Ibid., p. 108.

[91] Ibid., p. 113.

[92] Ibid., p. 123.

[93] Ibid., p. 134.

[94] Lawrence Wrightsman, _Social Psychology_, p. 270.

[95] Ibid., p. 271.

[96] Lawrence Kohlberg, "Stages of Moral Development as a Basis for Moral Education," pp. 43, 49; idem, "From Is To Ought," pp. 193-194.

[97] Lawrence Kohlberg, "Stages of Moral Development," p. 35.

[98] Ibid., pp. 86-88.

[99] Ibid., p. 36. Kohlberg often refers to the structure of moral reasoning as the _form_ of moral reasoning.

[100] Kohlberg, "From Is To Ought," p. 186.

[101] Ibid., p. 186.

[102] Kohlberg, "Stages of Moral Development," p. 79.

[103] Kohlberg, "From Is To Ought," p. 194.

[104] Kohlberg, "Stages of Moral Development," p. 47.

[105] Richard Duska and M. Whelan, Moral Development: A Guide to Piaget and Kohlberg, p. 44.

[106] Elliot Turiel, "Conflict and Transition in Adolescent Development," p. 18.

[107] Kohlberg, "Stages of Moral Development," p. 47.

[108] Kohlberg, "From Is To Ought," p. 196.

[109] Kohlberg, "Stages of Moral Development," p. 91.

[110] Ibid., p. 36.

[111] Ibid., p. 37.

[112] Ibid., p. 91.

[113] Ibid.

[114] Kohlberg, "From Is To Ought," p. 164.

[115] Ibid., p. 200.

[116] Ibid.

[117] Kohlberg, "From Is To Ought," pp. 204-206; idem, "Stages of Moral Development," p. 62.

[118] Kohlberg, "Stages of Moral Development," pp. 62-64.

[119] Kohlberg, "From Is To Ought," p. 208.

[120] Buhler, p. 144.

[121] Kohlberg, "Stages of Moral Development," p. 72.

[122] Ibid., p. 72.

[123] Ibid., pp. 46, 48.

[124] Ibid., p. 79.

[125] Ibid., p. 78.

[126] Ibid., p. 46.

[127] Ibid.

[128] This correlation fails because the notions of prescriptivity and universality do not admit of degrees: either a judgment is universal or it is not; similarly for prescriptivity. Hence to say that judgments become more prescriptive or universal does not make sense.

[129] Kohlberg, "Stages of Moral Development," p. 63.

[130] Ibid., p. 62.

[131] Epicurus, "Principal Doctrines," p. 82.

[132] J. C. C. Smart, Utilitarianism: For and Against, pp. 71-72, 42-57, 12.

[133] Of course, a theory of rule utilitarianism could be constructed that prohibits all civil disobedience. My point is that civil disobedience can be justified within some forms of rule utilitarianism.

[134] John Rawls, "Justification of Civil Disobedience," pp. 248-252.

[135] Kohlberg, "Stages of Moral Development," p. 63.

[136] Ibid., p. 36.

CHAPTER 3

THERAPY AND MORALITY: A RATIONAL APPROACH

3.0 Introduction

In the last chapter the attempt to use Kohlberg's theory to solve the problem of value adoption in therapy failed. In 3.1 I will show what went wrong with that attempt, and suggest a better one, by comparing Kohlberg's notion of indoctrination to the analysis of indoctrination presented in 2.1. I will argue that the best way to avoid indoctrination is to emphasize reasons, and that Kohlberg's work shows that this is a realistic way to deal with the problem. This is because certain aspects of moral development are rational.

However, to say that moral development is rational can be misleading. In 3.2 I suggest three ways in which a person's morality could be construed as rational. But what about the non-rational factors that have traditionally been included in moral development, such as emotions and habits? In 3.2.1 I argue that there is no conceptual incompatibility between Kohlberg's theory of moral judgment and the importance of emotions or habits in moral development. Kohlberg's failure to recognize this is what leads him to adopt a formal theory of ethics and the view that being moral consists in making certain sorts of judgments.

In 3.2.2 I examine the theory of morality on which psychoanalysis relies. I argue that just as Kohlberg ignores the behavioral aspect of being moral by concentrating on the development of moral judgment, psychoanalysts overlook the rational aspects of morality by concentrating on emotion. The failure of analysts to realize the cognitive aspects of morality keeps them from realizing that the way they propose handling client values in therapy, the value-free approach, is based on a cognitive theory of morality. Hence their official view of morality is quite different from the conception of morality which they actually employ.

In section 3.3 I will show that the official analytic and cognitive conceptions of morality do not merely differ with respect to the place of rationality in morality, but also in their views about the point, or nature, of morality. The analytic view, as mentioned in 2.2, sees morality as an alien, limiting force. Even when moral rules have been internalized and become part of a person, this is explained as a way that one is limited by morality without being aware of it. We "want" to do what is moral, but this "want" is artificial, a product of social pressure. Kohlberg, on the other hand, sees moral development as an integral part of personal development. Our moral system incorporates the way we understand our social environment and our relation to it. Morality is still restrictive, and necessarily so, but it also enters into how we direct ourselves in non-conflict situations. This is followed in 3.3.1 by a short discussion about the moral and non-moral issues in therapy.

Finally, in 3.4 I will argue that more adequate conceptions of indoctrination and morality, together with an adequate view of moral development, suggests a solution to the problem of therapeutic and therapist values in therapy. This is not to say that there will be no problems for a therapist, but only that there is a way of approaching these problems which is not doomed from the very beginning.

3.1 Kohlberg's Analysis of Indoctrination

In the preceding chapter, we saw that Kohlberg failed to show that promoting stage progression is not indoctrinative. Hence, cognitive moral education could not be justified in education or therapy. We cannot infer from this, however, that promoting stage progression is indoctrinative. If we could show that Kohlberg's arguments to justify moral development do not really attack the issue of indoctrination, then the failure of these arguments will have to be reconsidered. In this section I will argue that Kohlberg has misunderstood the problem of indoctrination. I will then go on to suggest what a more adequate justification of the cognitive model of moral development should look like.

Kohlberg never explicitly states how he understands indoctrination, but the kinds of solutions he offers are good indicators of what he thinks about it. In 2.3.2 we discussed three of Kohlberg's arguments to show that promoting stage progression is justified. In that section we saw that one kind of justification, that people develop morally as a result of trying to understand their environment, is not relevant to the problem of indoctrination. A person's natural tendencies could be used to further indoctrination as well as prevent it. What I will do now is examine the relevance of the other justifications to the problem of indoctrination. I will restate these justifications, and then see if the conceptions of indoctrination on which they are based are viable.

> 1) A person's stage, in itself, does not determine how a problem will be solved. Since stages are not correlated with any specific tendencies, there is nothing which can be said to be indoctrinated.

2) Given any stage, it is morally
   superior to any prior stage. Hence,
   advancing stage progression is not
   indoctrinative.

The first justification focuses upon the
problem of direct moral influence. Since no
direct influence is possible in determining the
nature of a stage, stage progression is not due
to indoctrination. I attacked this argument in
2.3.2 by showing that specific tendencies could
be associated with a stage. Stage progression,
then, could be used to promote specific moral
attitudes. But in arguing that way I did not
challenge the adequacy of this view of indoctrination. Is it true that direct moral influence
is indoctrinative in education and therapy? In
order to show that this is an inadequate conception of indoctrination, I will construct an
example to show that direct influence need not
be indoctrinative.

Suppose that a person, A, brings the following problem to a teacher or therapist, B. A
explains that his wife has run off with his best
friend, C. Understandably, A takes C's action
as a violation of their friendship. A's solution
to this, however, is to murder C. What should
B do in his role as advisor? Is this a case
where directly influencing A's beliefs would be
indoctrinative? It seems clear that B could
justifiably attempt to change A's belief that
C should be murdered. B could give plenty of
reasons, prudential and moral, why killing C is
wrong. B could urge A to think about the
consequences of murder, such as life imprison-
ment or, at best, the constant fear of being
caught. B could also ask A whether the punishment fits C's crime. Should running off with
the wife of a best friend be punishable by
death? Would A, if he were in B's place, think
that a just punishment? These are all questions
that could reasonably be asked of A. Which
questions would be stressed would depend on A.

The goal of the advisor is to <u>directly influence</u> A's judgment that C should be killed. In spite of this, B is not trying to indoctrinate A, but to give him good reasons for altering a belief.

This example shows that direct influence need not be indoctrinative. In 2.3.2 we showed how indirect influence, in the form of promoting stage progression, could be indoctrinative. It is, therefore, not possible to explain legitimate and illegitimate value influence in terms of the direct-indirect influence distinction. This is what we would expect if we look back to our analysis of indoctrination in 2.1. We analyzed indoctrination by what a teacher or therapist attempts to do: get another to adopt certain beliefs regardless of the reasons for those beliefs. The case of direct influence described above was not indoctrinative becuase B tried to give good reasons why his advice was sound.[137] The case of indirect influence described in 2.3.2 was indoctrinative because the teacher was attempting to use stage progression to encourage the adoption of select beliefs, regardless of the reasons for those beliefs. Kohlberg's argument rests on an inadequate understanding of indoctrination. Hence, the failure of Kohlberg's argument, which is based on the faulty conception, does not show that promoting stage progression is <u>not</u> justifiable.

Kohlberg's second reason for claiming that stage progression is not indoctrinative is that the later stages are morally superior to earlier ones. This can't be a way to avoid indoctrination, however, since it seems clear that most moral theories could be taught in indoctrinative and non-indoctrinative ways. Consider a rule utilitarian theory. One way of teaching this theory would be to present it as a reasonable way to organize our moral judgments, to explain the moral institutions that we have, and as an acceptable way to guide our personal relations with others. These points could be illustrated by examples showing how and why the theory works. Such teaching could also investigate certain problems utilitarian theory has, such as the problem of justice. Attempts could be made to explain our sense of justice in terms of utility. Finally, the teacher could urge utilitarianism as the best moral system, in spite of its problems. The goal of the teacher is not to indoctrinate, but to present rule utilitarianism as a reasonable theory.

Rule utilitarianism could also be taught with the intention to indoctrinate. A teacher could emphasize the importance of rules, and deride any theory that did not stress this. In doing so, the indoctrinative teacher could use many of the reasons the non-indoctrinative teacher used. The difference would be in what they are trying to do: the indoctrinative teacher is trying to instill certain beliefs, say, because he has been hired to do that. He uses reasons selectively to make sure that everything he says and does supports the adoption of a rule utilitarian moral view. His goal is not to make a good case for rule utilitarianism, but to get the students to become rule utilitarians.

Although this is a fanciful example, one thing is clear: the soundness of the theory being taught is not always important in deciding whether that theory is being indoctrinated. In the example concerning rule utilitarianism, the difference (consistent with our analysis in 2.1) was in what the teachers were trying to achieve: the first teacher, a proponent of rule utilitarianism, tried to build a reasoned case for the theory; there was an emphasis on why it is reasonable to adopt that theory. The second teacher's objective was to instill utilitarianism independently of the justification of that theory. Once again we see that Kohlberg relies on a faulty view of indoctrination.

Although I argued in 2.3.2 that Kohlberg's justifications for promoting moral development failed, we have just seen that his justifications do not really apply to the problem of indoctrination. Hence, we cannot assume that Kohlberg's work cannot significantly contribute to a solution to the problem of indoctrination or its therapeutic counterpart. On our preferred analysis of indoctrination, the distinction between legitimate and illegitimate moral influence depends on whether the emphasis is on a particular moral view or the reasonableness of that view. Given this analysis, Kohlberg's work shows that this is a difference that makes a difference; emphasizing reasons can have an effect that is different from emphasizing a particular doctrine. The non-cognitive view of moral development, as we saw in 2.2, cannot countenance this distinction.

We should be clear about how this approach applies to our therapeutic problem. It shows that moral values can be discussed in therapy without necessarily being adopted by a client. We can see how that this is a justifiable approach that is independent of the ethical viability of any stage and of direct influence. I am not arguing that the moral soundness of a stage makes no difference. What I am suggesting is that the best way for a person to examine his moral reasoning is by concentrating on the way beliefs are justified. Nor does this solution suggest that direct influence is always justified. We have only noted that eliminating direct influence will not eliminate the problem of indoctrination or the problem of uncritical value adoption in therapy.

One way to describe Kohlberg's contribution, then, is that he has shown that reasons, or rational considerations, play a significant role in moral development. We cannot fully assess this contribution, however, until we better understand the claim that morality and moral development is rational.

3.2 Rationality and Morality

Our discussion so far has stressed that the
presence of rational elements in moral development shows that moral value adoption can be a
critical process. We have taken this to show
that the moral values expressed in therapy can
be critically evaluated by a client. But, what
does it mean to say that moral development is
rational? Does this rule out all non-rational
elements in moral development? That is, is it
possible that moral development has non-rational
features which a therapist could influence?
Finally, what do claims about moral development
show about the nature of morality or what it is
to be a moral person? Can we infer that morality
has a certain feature because moral development
does?

In this section I will look at what Kohlberg
means when he says that moral development is
rational. In 3.2.1 I will argue that Kohlberg's
theory is compatible with postulating non-
rational factors in moral development.
Kohlberg's failure to consider this seriously
results in an inadequate notion of morality and
what it is to be moral. In 3.2.2 I will argue
that psychoanalysts also mistakenly infer a
theory of morality from a theory of moral
development. I will argue that psychoanalysts,
despite their pronouncements to the contrary,
rely on a cognitive view of morality.

When Kohlberg argues that cognitive
elements help to determine the formation of a
person's moral system, he means at least three
(connected) things: that moral development has
a cognitive basis, that moral judgments are the
kinds of things for which reasons can be given,
and that moral feelings are determined by a
cognitive appraisal of the situation giving rise
to those feelings.

We have seen how at least one kind of moral development, that which incorporates structural change, results from a growing understanding of the social environment and the place of an individual within that environment. A moral conceptual structure is retained only as long as it explains the moral environment and serves as an effective guide for action. This theory of development accounts for data, such as cross-cultural regularity, better than competing non-cognitive theories. Further support of this theory is that the cognitive method of moral education is in many cases effective. That is, direct application of this theory to education supports the view that cognitive factors play a crucial role in moral development.

Coupled with this is the view that moral judgments are the kinds of things which admit of justification. Moral judgments are not just a matter of taste, but are things for which people often have reasons. To see the truth of this we need only look more closely at what Kohlberg means by 'structure'. As we saw, a person's moral structure is determined by the way specific moral judgments are justified. That is, to have a moral structure _is_ to give certain kinds of reasons for one's moral convictions. This fits in with the claim that "content" learned from the environment is cognitively mediated. What this means, at least in part, is that a specific belief has to fit into the justificatory system that a person has. As we saw, this cognitive mediation can have an effect on when a rule is applied: a stage 1 individual could justify stealing in situations where one does not get caught, whereas a stage 5 individual could not. We do not need to accept a fullblown stage theory to concede this point. All we have to do is understand that there are various ways that people can and do interpret moral codes, and that that interpretation has a significant effect on when the code is invoked or followed.

Consistent with the cognitive view that reasons can be given for moral judgments is Kohlberg's rejection of the thesis that moral judgments are based upon, or arise out of emotions. Kohlberg says:

> the cognitive-developmental view holds that "cognition" and "affect" are different aspects of . . . the same mental events, that all mental events have both cognitive and affective aspects, and that the development of mental dispositions reflects structural changes recognizable in both cognitive and affective perspectives.[138]

Although Kohlberg seems to give both cognition and affect equal roles, in another passage he makes clear that cognition is basic:

> . . . the primary psychological referent of the term "moral" is a judgment, not a behavior or an affect, for example, "guilt." (The difference between fear or anxiety on the one hand and guilt on the other is provided only by a concept of moral judgments associated with the affect, not with the affect itself.)[139]

Moral feelings are rational because they are dependent on judgments for which an agent has reasons. Guilt, for example, is dependent on a belief that we have done, are planning, or want to do something morally wrong. Those people who cannot help but feel guilt for an action or intention, even though they do not think that act or intention is wrong, pose a problem. However, it is interesting to note that such feelings of guilt are often attributed to a repressed super-ego evaluation or to the person displacing the guilt from one act or intention to another. These kinds of explanations support the view that a moral emotion, such as guilt, is based upon a judgment.

94

What do the above considerations show about non-cognitive factors, e.g., habits or emotions such as sympathy? Does Kohlberg show that these non-rational factors are unimportant? That is, can therapists simply forget about the non-rational aspects of moral influence? Kohlberg's work at times seems to imply this. In the next section I will try to show that this inference is not warranted.

3.2.1 Cognitive and Non-cognitive Factors in Moral Development

In 3.2 we briefly discussed what it means to say that moral development is a rational, cognitive process. In this section I want to urge that this does not rule out that non-cognitive elements or processes may be essential to moral development. I will argue that Kohlberg's failure to recognize this fully has led, in part, to his forming inadequate conceptions of morality and of what it is to be a moral person.

The first place to look for the necessity of non-cognitive elements in moral development is Kohlberg's own theory. Kohlberg himself notes that cognitive abilities alone are insufficient to explain moral judgment:

> . . . moral judgment is not simply the application of intelligence in the sense of logical-technological thought to moral situations and problems.[140]

The missing ingredient is the ability to take the role of another which requires "sympathy or concern for welfare consequences to others."[141] Again,

> Our point is that concern for the welfare of other beings, "empathy," or "role-taking," is the precondition for experiencing a moral conflict.[142]

Hence, it is clear that these non-cognitive factors are necessary for moral development: without them we could not fully understand the nature of a moral conflict. Of course, being sympathetic or empathetic is not sufficient for cognitive moral development. Also, the intensity of our sympathetic feelings is determined to some degree by our cognitive moral system; a stage 3 individual should tend to feel more sympathetic towards family members, for example. This does not mean that our caring for others is a product of understanding alone. Kohlberg admits this in the quote above when he denies that moral judgment is based solely on cognitive appraisal.

There is, therefore, room in a cognitive theory of moral development for emotions such as sympathy and empathy. Can we make the same point about character traits that we just made about emotions? Two purported features of character traits are important here: that they are general ways of acting (i.e., all kinds of situations are dealt with in similar ways) and that they are non-rational responses to situations. If we pay careful attention to this distinction, we will see that character traits can be fit into cognitive moral development.

My first two arguments will deal with the claim that traits are non-rational responses to situations. First, I will show that even on an extreme non-cognitive conception of traits, traits could play a crucial role in a theory of cognitive moral development. Second, I will show that traits, at least as ethical theorists usually construe them, have significant cognitive components. Finally, I attack Kohlberg's strongest argument against traits, that there is no generality of behavior of the kind required for traits. His argument would imply that character traits do not exist. I will show that the evidence he presents is insufficient to support such a strong claim.

One reason Kohlberg objects to traits is that they are learned in a non-rational way. This is presumably incompatible with a theory of moral development which is based on cognitive factors. This is a conceptual argument: the kind of moral development Kohlberg proposes is incompatible with an account of moral development that relies on traits.

The following is a conceptually coherent picture of moral development which refutes this alleged incompatibility. Aristotle suggested that the soul has three parts, one rational and two irrational.[143] Only one of the irrational parts of the soul--the appetitive part, which is the seat of many wants and desires--is subject to direct rational control. Aristotle accounts for our ability to control our desires in the appetitive soul by habituation. He says, "we become just by doing just acts, temperate by doing temperate acts, brave by doing brave acts,"[144] and further, "being habituated to feel fear or confidence, we become brave or cowardly."[145] Aristotle clearly sees habit development as an essential part of acquiring a trait such as bravery. This leaves open the question, however, of how such __habits__ are acquired (i.e., the habits which contribute to the formation of character traits). It may be that in order to become habituated to feel confident, we must choose the relevant acts for the right reason. Repeating acts by accident or through coercion may not be the kind of repetition that will contribute to developing the virtue of bravery.[146] Let us suppose, though, that mere repetition of the appropriate acts, for whatever reason, will lead to the development of a trait. Is this incompatible with a cognitive theory of moral development such as Kohlberg's? I think not. We must keep in mind that Kohlberg's theory deals with the development of moral judgment; hence, we could construe Kohlberg's work as an elucidation of our moral __conceptual__ development. Progress through the stages could be interpreted as gaining more adequate criteria by which to judge our traits.

Even though traits (as non-rational responses to situations) can be fit into a cognitive theory of moral development, must we think that moral character traits, at least as many ethicists think of them, are essentially non-rational? Consider the virtue of courage. James Wallace has suggested the following conditions for a courageous act:

> (a) A believes that it is dangerous for him to do Y.
>
> (b) A believes that his doing Y is worth the risks it involves.
>
> (c) A believes that it is possible for him not to do Y.
>
> (d) The danger A sees in doing Y must be sufficiently formidable that most people would find it difficult to do Y.
>
> (e) A is not coerced into doing Y by threats of punishment, which he fears more than the dangers of doing Y.[147]

I do not want to explain or to defend all aspects of these conditions here. I am, rather, offering it as a model of how we would go about determining whether an act is courageous. These conditions include cognitive elements such as the necessity that a person judge his act to be worthwhile. A dangerous act done on the basis of a whim, for example, would be foolish, not courageous. This means that the courageousness of an act depends upon a person assessing a situation as one requiring a dangerous act. Conditions a and c describe other cognitive factors required for an act's courageousness.

To act in a courageous way, then, requires more than a non-rational response to a situation. It requires that we understand both the kind of situation that it is, and that that kind of situation makes a dangerous act worth the risk.

We have been discussing the courageousness of acts. What is it for a person to be courageous or, in other words, to have courage as a virtue (trait)? Well, it is merely to respond regularly to appropriate situations in a courageous way. How often such situations must arise and how many need to be reacted to courageously for a person to be courageous is difficult to determine.[148] This issue, however, is different from the issue of the role of cognition in moral virtues. If virtues such as honesty and courage do rely on cognitive appraisal, as surely they must, then Kohlberg's theory is directly relevant to a moral trait theory. Kohlberg's work could be used to show how we come to better understand which situations require a response and why that response is justified or perhaps obligatory. In fact, a moral trait theory that incorporates cognition would have to rely upon some theory as to how we come to develop our conceptual abilities.

This leaves us with the last of Kohlberg's objections to trait theories, viz., that traits do not exist. Clearly, if Kohlberg can show that traits do not exist, their compatibility with his theory will mean nothing. Kohlberg's major argument for the non-existence of traits is the study by Hartshorne and May which examined the effect of traditional methods of moral education on such traits as "deception, helpfulness, cooperation, persistence and inhibition."[149] "Traditional methods of education" refers to the praising of traits, praising those who possess those traits, urging children to develop those traits and providing good examples. They studied children who were educated in this way at home, church, school, Sunday schools and

99

clubs.[150]   Two conclusions of the study are of
interest here. The first is that there was no
significant correlation between traditional modes
of training and virtuous behavior, and second,
what they found were not general ways of approaching situations, but rather responses to specific
kinds of situations. Regarding the first
conclusion, Hartshorne and May say:

> A virtue approach to moral education is
> fruitless and may be harmful if it flies
> in the face of what the child sees as
> "working" in the situations he finds
> himself.[151]

Not only is there no positive correlation between
a traditional virtue approach to moral education
and development of those virtues, there is
evidence that such methods of education may be
negatively correlated with developing the virtues.
With respect to the generality of habits
Hartshorne and May say:

> It seems to be a fair conclusion from
> our data that honest and deceptive
> tendencies represent not general
> traits, nor action guided by general
> ideals, but specific habits learned in
> relation to specific situations which
> have made the one or the other mode of
> response successful.[152]

This study and others similar to it convinced Kohlberg of the inadequacy of traits for
explaining moral behavior. We must be careful,
however, in how we interpret Hartshorne and May's
conclusions. We must remember that they studied
children of grade school age. A trait theory
need not predict consistency at this early age.
Also, Hartshorne and May were not studying
highly trained teachers. It could be that a
better method would yield more consistent
behavior. In fact, Hartshorne and May suggest
what a better method would be like. They

emphasize concentrating on specific habits. So, for example, if it could be shown that there are basic <u>kinds</u> of situations in which one has opportunities to cheat, non-cheating behavior could be taught in those kinds of situations. This would result in a general tendency not to cheat. One way to use Hartshorne and May's study, then, is to increase the effectiveness of habit training by concentrating on situational variables. We need not completely reject the notion of general traits.

What I want to suggest now is that even the evidence for moral behavior being situationally specific does not show that moral traits, as Aristotle, Dewey, Wallace and others conceive them, do not exist. That is, I want to argue that the truth of:

> You cannot divide the world into honest and dishonest people. Almost everyone cheats some of the time; cheating is distributed in a bell curve around a level of moderate cheating.[153]

does not imply that there are no honest or dishonest people. An analogous example would be the attempt to divide the world into two colors, black and white. Most things would not fall into either category, but would be distributed across the gray scale. We could not infer, however, that nothing is black or white. Nor, if for some reason one color was better suited to the environment than another, would it be ridiculous to attempt to "promote" the desired color.

With respect to moral characteristics, such as honesty, some of the same considerations apply. For example, if cheating is distributed in a bell curve as Kohlberg suggests, what are we to say about those at the extreme ends of that curve? Is it not likely that they are the persons we would characterize as honest or dishonest? And surely the fact that even the most honest cheat once in a while does not show they are not honest. To have a virtue like honesty, one need not react to _every_ situation honestly. An honest person must react honestly most of the time, and perhaps always in very important and demanding cases. This still leaves room, though, for occasional acts of dishonesty.

So it seems that Kohlberg's arguments do not show that moral traits do not exist. To understand further why those arguments fail we must examine why moral theorists would rely on traits. The most fundamental reason why moral philosophers have given traits an important place in moral development is because traits represent regular and therefore predictable patterns of behavior. Our dealings with others are partly guided by how we judge them on moral terms. It is important to know if others are truthful, or prone to cheat. We would be very wary of doing business with a person who is a notorious liar and embezzler. Hence, one of the moral aspects of others we need to know is what they are likely to do in moral situations.

Another important aspect of traits is that they are the kind of things that are often exhibited unreflectively. Honesty is a good example of this: the honest person does not constantly reflect about situations to determine if he should be honest. Rather, honesty would be the usual, unreflective way of dealing with most situations. The unreflective nature of having a trait is important since we would have time for little else if we reflected about every situation. Further, some situations require immediate action, not allowing time to reflect. And, to go back to the point about predictability, this unreflective mode of moral behavior would seem to enhance consistent behavior. However, to say that virtuous behavior is often unreflective is not to say that that behavior is non-cognitive or unjustifiable. Stage development (at least through the first 4 stages) is unreflective, yet it is a rational and, Kohlberg claims, a justifiable process.

Kohlberg, however, concentrates on a different aspect of moral development, viz., the reasons or principles that people have which help motivate them to act in moral ways. By concentrating on moral reasoning, he often under-emphasizes not only the role of moral behavior in moral development, but the importance of people regularly, or usually acting in moral ways. As we saw, Kohlberg's official view with respect to moral regularity was that such regularity is a myth. Kohlberg himself, though, cites studies which suggest that consistent moral behavior is positively correlated with higher stages. As I mentioned previously, in a study by Milgram where subjects were induced to believe that they were inflicting pain on another volunteer subject, only 13% of stages 1-5 refused to inflict the pain, whereas 75% of stage 6 subjects refused.[154] Krebs found in his study that while 75% of children in stages 1-4 cheated, only 20% in stages 5 and 6 cheated.[155] For college age students, it was found that only 11% of those in stages 5 and 6 cheated while 42% of those in lower stages cheated.[156] What these studies show is that there is a consistent response to a problem among persons in the same stage. This suggests (but does not prove) that we would find that persons at higher stages would consistently act in moral ways in such situations.

In fact, that we find virtuous behavior, that is, regular moral behavior of certain types, associated with the higher stages is a necessary condition for morally justifying those stages. If the higher stages were associated with lying or non-benevolence or, less radically, with general unpredictability, this would be prima facie reason to think that higher stages cannot be morally justified. Of course there could be ways to explain this anomaly; that is why it is a _prima facie_ reason.

What I have been trying to show is that the important insights of theories of morality that emphasize virtues cannot be ignored in theories of moral development or in ethical theorizing. The view of a moral person as one who acts in regular ways thus enabling others to reliably predict his behavior is a crucial moral fact. This insight is not vitiated by the fact that many people do not act in these regular ways. Kohlberg objected to trait theories on the grounds that this regularity is founded upon non-rational, unjustifiable, mechanical responses to situations, much like nail biting. I have argued that the notion of traits as used by ethical theorists is neither non-rational nor intrinsically unjustifiable. Consider, for example, Dewey's conception of moral habit. For Dewey (who speaks of both intellectual and behavioral habits), an important aspect of a proper moral habit is its flexibility in adapting to novel situations. Habits are modified by past experience. Dewey explicitly rejects the view that habits are characteristically repetitious.[157] It is possible, then, to understand a trait theory of moral development as the behavioral complement of Kohlberg's theory of the development of moral judgment. That is, Kohlberg's work can be seen as showing the reasoning most likely to lead to regular moral behavior.

What I have been trying to show is that there is a reasonable conception of character traits to which Kohlberg can agree. Once we see that the possession of traits such as honesty or courage requires cognitive appraisal (though not necessarily reflective appraisal) and that it is not a necessary condition for having a virtue that a person exhibit that virtue in _every_ appropriate situation, traits can be conceived as the behavioral manifestations of

moral reasoning. Of course Kohlberg's attack on
traits was based on a completely different view
of what a trait is. He conceived of them as
essentially non-rational, and rejected them for
that reason. As we saw, that rejection led him
to underestimate the importance of behavior in
moral development. Kohlberg has shown, however,
that to understand moral development fully we
need to study moral reasoning. A complete theory
of moral development must integrate what people
do with why they do it. To predict a person's
behavior reliably, we need to know both factors.

It is important that we understand how reason
and action are linked in the moral sphere. A
therapist who affects a client's moral reasoning
has worries which go beyond violating the client's
right to "think for himself." The therapist, in
helping effect changes in a client's reasoning
is having an effect on the client's moral behavior
as well. This fact makes it evident that therapists should try to understand the process of
moral development and, further, that they should
have a general idea about the nature of morality.
All too often those who study moral acquisition
make simple inferences from what they consider
to be the mainspring of moral development to the
nature of morality. Kohlberg, in emphasizing
moral judgment, attempts to ground morality
entirely on features of judgment: his use of
formalism is the most apparent instance of this.
He is led thus to underestimate the importance
of behavior in moral development, as is evidenced
in his statement that judgment is the only kind
of thing which is properly moral.[158] From the
point of view being developed here, the important
contribution of virtue theorists is not their
attempt to explain human behavior in terms of
internal mechanisms, but their emphasis on how
people regularly act.

Psychoanalysts, at least in their official
pronouncements, make a similar error on the side

of emotion. They explain moral development primarily in terms of emotional identification and feelings such as guilt and shame. They are often led to the conclusion that morality is nothing more than a set of emotional attitudes adopted from the social environment. This conception of morality, and how it is connected to the theory of psychoanalysis, is the subject of the next section.

3.2.2 Psychoanalysis and Morality

In the preceding section we saw that Kohlberg erroneously inferred that only cognitive aspects of morality (i.e., judgments) were moral because moral development has significant cognitive aspects. Psychoanalysts make a similar mistake: since they describe moral development primarily in terms of non-cognitive emotional elements, they tend to construe morality as a set of non-cognitive, emotional attitudes. In this section I will offer an explanation of why they make this mistake. I will argue that analytic arguments are not directed against morality per se, but inadequate moral systems. On this basis I will show that many therapists covertly rely upon a cognitive theory of morality.

Analysts overtly adopt a non-cognitive view of morality because of their conception of moral development and their related theory of neurosis. In 2.2 we saw that the analytic theory of moral acquisition is based on non-rational, emotional forces. We adopt the moral system of those with whom we identify. As we grow, we adopt the values which we find in society. Of course, we do not adopt all the values we discover there; but the method by which we adopt some and not other values is not rational. The analytic theory of neurosis fits this explanation of moral development. Debilitating neurosis is the result of internalizing values that are antithetical to our nature, thus creating demands we cannot meet. The inability to meet these demands results in guilt, anxiety and depression. In healthy moral development one still adopts values antithetical to one's nature instincts, but one is able to redirect (sublimate) natural instincts into socially acceptable forms.[159] Morality is thought of as a system of rules which restrict otherwise desirable behavior. The healthy person is able to redirect his desires and thus avoid guilt and anxiety. The unhealthy person still fights against moral restrictions, and suffers guilt as a consequence.

Given their theory of moral development, and the potentially destructive nature of being moral, it is not surprising that many analysts view morality as a non-rational, destructive, force. However, this inference from the nature of moral development to the nature of morality is not warranted. The fact that a person adopts a belief or set of beliefs in a non-rational way does not imply that those beliefs cannot be justified. A non rational mode of belief acquisition proves nothing in regard to the justification of the beliefs acquired. So, even if the analysts are correct about how we acquire our moral standards, it could still be the case that these standards are justified. What we need to know, then, is whether a sound argument to show that personal moral systems are generally harmful or unjustified can be developed within an analytic framework. James Gilligan, a psychiatrist, addresses himself to this task in "Beyond Morality."[160] His article not only illustrates the kind of mistakes that non-cognitive theories can make, but also shows how an unhealthy value system can affect an individual.

Gilligan begins his article, "Beyond Morality," by stating that morality has been killed by its own excessive self-examination that has been going on since the eighteenth century.[161] He attempts to characterize morality, show how it

fails and suggest a healthier substitute for it.
Concerning the nature of morality, Gilligan
associates it with actions that we are compulsed
or obligated to do, as opposed to actions which
are done from love.[162] More specifically he
claims that morality is:

> . . . the motivating of behavior by the
> moral emotions of shame or guilt and the
> cognitive structuring of social situa-
> tions in terms of moral ("ought" and
> "should") rather than in terms of
> scientific ideas (psychological under-
> standing).[163]

It is clear, then, that Gilligan's statement
about the death of morality is tied to an analysis
of morality in terms of moral emotions, of which
there are two basic kinds, shame and guilt. But
then what can he mean by "morality is dead"?
Are shame and guilt dead, or have they ceased to
exist? No, Gilligan's claim is that they should
be eliminated; although he believes that these
emotions serve an essential developmental function, the goal is to go beyond them.[164]

To fully understand his claim about morality,
then, we need to know more about shame and guilt.
Since Gilligan identifies guilt as the "highest
stage of moral development,"[165] I will concentrate
on it. Gilligan defines guilt as:

> . . . the feeling of having committed
> a sin, a crime, . . . the feeling of
> culpability; the feeling of obligation;
> the feeling of being dangerous . . .
> to others; and the feeling of needing
> expiation and deserving punishment.[166]

Gilligan wants to eliminate these feelings
because he sees them, along with shame, as the
root of many emotional disturbances. He cites
six case histories where shame, guilt, or both,
are intimately connected with atrocities to

oneself and others. To show why a therapist
would want to eliminate shame and guilt, I will
cite one of these case histories in which
Gilligan describes a psychotic depressive driven
by guilt.

> . . . soon after one woman's psychotic
> depression lifted she elaborated a
> phantasy about a cannabalistic child
> who ate his playmates and killed his
> mother. When she was not depressed, she
> liked to bite her husband, often severe-
> ly, when making love. She also punished
> herself for her oral sadism by turning
> it into an oral masochism: She nearly
> starved herself to death; and the
> sexual act she found most gratifying
> (and from which she reached orgasm)
> was manipulating her nipples with pins,
> causing pain and bleeding, while she
> imagined that a sadistic starving Nazi
> General was getting milk from them by
> biting them.[167]

I quote this at length because Gilligan
offers five other examples, equally powerful,
where guilt and shame are claimed to be at the
root of the illness. His analysis of this case
is that the extreme guilt felt by the woman is
what motivated her to hurt herself and eventually
to attempt suicide, these actions being ways to
alleviate guilt. This seems to be a clear case
where guilt is "out of control"; it does not help
her avoid the acts which are the object of her
guilt, and the guilt in turn motivates her to act
in ways about which she feels guilty. It should
not be surprising that Gilligan, and therapists
in general, might come to see morality as a
destructive force, fostering illness and hinder-
ing recovery.[168]

How, though, do we go "beyond morality"?
Gilligan's answer is that the analyst should help

the client to replace questions about what he should do with questions about what he wants to do. Concerning the Heinz dilemma (presented in Chapter 2) Gilligan thinks the analyst "would ask Heinz what his hang-up over the issue of 'should' was all about, and he would wonder if Heinz were not asking himself what he 'should' do . . . as a way to avoid asking himself what is emotionally more threatening but cognitively more relevant, namely, 'What do I want to do, and why do I want to do it?'"[169]

Gilligan argues that this approach is not subject to Mowrer's worry mentioned in Chapter 1, viz., the possibility of creating egoistic or sociopathic individuals. Gilligan claims that eliminating a person's morality through therapy does not result in moral egoism; rather, it helps the individual go beyond moral altruism.[170] This is because the advancement beyond altruism is to a state in which the individual tries to create relationships in which the needs of all the relevant persons are satisfied as much as is possible.[171] We can now understand what Gilligan means when he says that psychological understanding should replace morality: by psychological understanding, he means love of self and others which is "directed toward the resolution of conflicts, the transcending of dilemmas, and the solving of problems."[172]

What should be said about Gilligan's argument? Surely we do not want to say that egoism, which "needlessly" sacrifices the interest of others to oneself, or altruism, which "needlessly" sacrifices self-interest to that of the group, is preferable to the kind of psychological understanding Gilligan proposes. And it is obvious in the case history cited above that guilt serves no good purpose at all. Since these are the major points of the argument that Gilligan proposes, are we then committed to rejecting morality?

It can be shown that we are not so committed
if we examine Gilligan's conception of morality.
What support is there for defining morality in
terms of feelings, such as shame and guilt? I
argued earlier that a feeling of guilt could not
be understood apart from a judgment that one has
done something wrong, or at least a desire or
resolution to do something wrong. A judgment,
on this analysis, is conceptually prior to the
feeling.[173] It cannot be argued that Gilligan
is using the term 'feeling' loosely in this
respect, since he explicitly distinguishes
judgment and feeling and asserts that moral
feelings are prior to the judgment.[174]

Although it may be true that a feeling of
guilt or shame may lead one to condemn oneself
or others using moral language, it is inconceivable
that guilt or shame could be the origin of all
moral judgments, since the way we identify a
feeling as one of guilt is in terms of a cognitive
appraisal of a certain state of affairs, viz.,
that we are doing or planning to do something we
judge to be morally wrong.[175]

Apart from the inadequate analysis of
morality in terms of guilt, the analysis of
guilt itself is unacceptable. Although it may be
correct to say that guilt is the feeling of
having committed a sin (although we can believe
that we have committed a sin, crime or the like,
without feeling guilty) or an injustice as
Gilligan does, is it also right to identify guilt
with a feeling of obligation or of being dangerous to others? Surely one can feel obligated
without feeling guilty, especially when one is
doing what one judges to be obligatory. It is
equally clear that one could feel dangerous to
others without feeling guilty if one thought,
say, that others deserved to be intimidated or
hurt. This objection is not merely concerned
with Gilligan's analysis of guilt; rather it
reveals a basic confusion which this type of
thinking often exhibits. When one sees serious

psychological problems that are associated with guilt feelings, and morality is analyzed in terms of guilt, there is a rejection of morality. This rejection of morality in turn implies a rejection of moral obligation.

If we concentrate on the cognitive aspect of morality, Gilligan's argument breaks down because we cannot analyze morality in terms of feelings alone. We feel obligated because we judge, correctly or incorrectly, that an action is obligatory. Guilt, then, only arises if we fail to do it, or plan or desire not to do it. Further, the reason that we could feel dangerous to others without feeling guilty is because of our judgment or belief that this feeling is justified. One analytic error, then, rests on neglecting the cognitive aspects of a person's morality, which results in analyzing moral phenomena entirely in terms of feelings.

If a client is suffering from severe guilt, the problem may be located in his judgment that he wants or is doing something immoral. Let us suppose that the woman mentioned in the case history above was raised by a parent who held that eating is morally wrong: one cannot avoid it; however, the goal is to eat as little as possible. The child's natural and inevitable feelings of hunger are punished by the parent, and eventually the child begins to feel guilty about her hunger. In this instance the guilt is excessive and interferes with the child's normal development. Gilligan can convincingly argue that this guilt is harmful and should be eliminated. This analytic diagnosis, though, is not based on the destructive nature of guilt, but on the fact that feelings of hunger are not the kinds of things about which one should feel guilty. If the child had been torturing a younger sister, for example, instead of merely being hungry, the guilt would not be out of place. Surely Gilligan does not want to say that torturing an innocent human being is

something we should be able to do without remorse.
So, we can agree with Gilligan and with therapists in general that many value systems may
indeed be destructive, but this does not entail
that it is the nature of moral value systems to
be destructive. In fact, Gilligan's arguments
to show the destructive nature of guilt employ
moral criteria concerning the proper objects of
guilt.

On this analysis, Gilligan's arguments show
the very opposite of what he intends; since the
handling of extreme cases of guilt will often
involve a conception of morality that rules the
guilt out of place, it is pointless to reject
morality. How does this affect Gilligan's
suggestion that we should go beyond morality?
On closer analysis, Gilligan's replacement for
morality is iteslf a moral system. Gilligan's
psychological understanding looks like a stage 5
or 6 conception of morality; it prescribes that
we solve problems maximizing the interest of all,
neither over nor under emphasizing personal or
group interest. Gilligan misses this in spite of
the fact that he is familiar with Kohlberg's
cognitive-developmental moral theory. This is
because of his analysis of morality in terms of
guilt and shame. He sees the moral stages as
showing the progression from shame to guilt:
Level I is associated with shame, Level II with
a mixture of shame and guilt, and Level III with
guilt alone.[176] This is why he says guilt
represents the highest moral emotion. Gilligan
wants to take Kohlberg's analysis of morality
as correct, but wants to deny that morality is of
any use to a person or society. Gilligan's
mistake, as I see it, is that he fails to
distinguish adequate from inadequate moral judgments, and this is because of his belief that
moral judgments are the result of irrational
feelings, and hence do not admit justification.

Gilligan, then, is relying on a preferred
conception of morality in order to show that

other moral systems are inadequate. Since he offers reasons for preferring his system of morality, he takes a cognitive approach to morality. Although this is just one article, I think that a similar reliance upon a cognitive theory of morality is true of many therapists and therapies. We can show the pervasiveness of cognitive interpretations of morality if we look at one of the common ways of handling client value problems: the value-free approach.

In order to give a cognitive analysis of the value-free method, I will briefly review its nature. It will be remembered that the value-free approach does not deny the presence of moral issues, the importance of these issues to the client, nor the importance of the way in which a client resolves these issues. The value-free method provides a way for a therapist to help a client work on moral issues without forcing him in any particular direction. To achieve this, a therapist is encouraged to do two things: a) to help the patient clarify his moral beliefs, reveal inconsistencies and examine how well the client's particular judgments (e.g., that he should ignore a plea for help) correlate with avowed beliefs (e.g., that one should help others) and b) to examine how these moral beliefs relate to the moral beliefs of others and how well they contribute to an understanding of the morality of other people and institutions (see 1.2). If we attend to the two activities that the value-free thesis proposes, we see they are just the ways a therapist is most likely to prompt moral change on the cognitive model of morality. This method of handling moral issues in therapy is one that is most likely to affect the structure of moral thought by digging out and concentrating on the different ways moral principles can be evaluated: are these beliefs consistent, do they explain the moral phenomena we experience? Not only is there this similarity, but if we compare the method of the value-free approach to the philosophical method of evaluating

114

moral theories, the same kind of point can be made. Two necessary conditions for the adequacy of moral theory are that it be consistent and that it explain the moral behavior of others as well as the morality of social institutions. This is not to say that a moral theory must support all behavior that is deemed "moral," or that it provide moral backing for each and every social institution; deciding what behavior and what institutions (or aspects of institutions) we take as important is a difficult and demanding task. My point here is that this is a way (and perhaps the only way) by which we can evaluate moral systems, and that it coincides both with the way Kohlberg conceives of the psychological mechanism of moral development and the solution analysts propose to handle the moral problems that clients present.

I would like to suggest that the congruence between the method of the value-free approach and the method a cognitive-developmental theory proposes is not coincidental. Despite the official psychoanalytic doctrine of morality as basically irrational, therapy is often a place where moral demands and beliefs are subjected to rational criteria. Clearly, any therapy that employs such criteria is assuming, whether the therapist is aware of it or not, that morality is the kind of thing that is subject to rational review. Gilligan sees the result of such review to be a rejection of morality. As we saw, his claim is flawed by his limit notion of morality. I want to make the same claim with respect to the value-free thesis as a whole. Its problem is that it identifies morality with very specific beliefs such as those regarding pre-marital sex, cheating on tests, lying to parents, etc. In their attempt to avoid these particular issues, analysts concentrate instead on much more power-ful moral issues such as the worth of an individual, the adequacy of egoism, and appeals to authority as ways to determine what is morally right. This attempt to avoid morality fails because of a

failure to recognize a significant aspect of a
person's morality, viz., how particular beliefs
relate to each other and to more basic principles.
This was the argument of 1.3.1, viz., that the
moral sphere cannot be avoided in therapy. It
is quite illuminating that the attempt to avoid
these particular moral issues led analysts to
concentrate on what a cognitive moral theory would
advocate; but this is what we should expect
since they both hold, implicitly and explicitly
(respectively), that moral issues are subject to
rational analysis. The non-cognitivism of the
value-free thesis, however, prevents the realization of such rational review as a method of moral
theorizing. On their limited view of morality,
they cannot see the connection between this
critical process and moral development: their
only recognized view of moral development leaves
no room for morality to develop apart from specific belief influence. Anything that does not fit
that model is not a case of moral influence.

What I have been attempting to argue is
that any method of therapy that concentrates on
"thinking things through," i.e., looking for and
examining reasons and motives for values,
implicitly holds that moral development admits
rational criticism no matter how strongly the
non-rationality of personal moral systems is
advocated. I have suggested that the reason for
rejecting rational influence in morality results
from identifying a person's morality with specific
beliefs. The advantage of the cognitive model
is that it enables us to understand the different
kinds of moral problems that a person has as
well as different ways a therapist can affect the
client's moral system.

In the next section I will examine further
the difference between non-cognitive and
cognitive conceptions of morality and moral
development. We will find that there are more
significant differences between these views than
in how they understand moral influence or moral

development.

3.3 One Function of Morality and Its Relation to Mental Health

In this section I will show that there are fundamental meta-ethical differences between cognitive and non-cognitive moral conceptions which further explain why non-cognitivists make the mistakes we have been discussing. In Chapter 2 I mentioned that the analytic non-cognitive view describes the function of morality as providing limits and restrictions for otherwise desirable behavior. Consider the moral command that one should keep one's promises. This rule, and the social and internal sanctions that back it up, are viewed as a way to force a person to do what he says in the event that breaking his promise promotes his self-interest more than keeping it. Without such rules Freud speculated that society would collapse: the free reign of aggressive and sexual impulses would destroy all trust between people. Social-learning theorists may not employ instincts in this Freudian fashion, but their basic view of morality is the same: a set of rules which limits personally desirable behavior. Morality is described as a foreign element imposed on a person from without. One gets the impression that morality is a necessary evil[177] and that a person could fully develop without any moral convictions at all. This is suggested by the way they construe morality: they seem to suppose that a person has a set of desires, feelings and goals, and that morality is there to approve or reject them. Cognitive-developmental theory, on the other hand, sees morality primarily as a system for understanding our social environment and our place in it. This is not to say that morality loses its "restrictive nature," but only that our judgment that we should restrict ourselves in certain ways is a function of general views about our roles in our social

117

environment. On this view, morality plays an
integral part in personal development. Hence,
one's morality does not merely function to
restrict things we wish to do, but also enters
into our decisions about what we <u>want</u> to do.
That is, the cognitive model, as <u>I am</u> interpreting
it, sees one's goals and aspirations as being
partially determined by one's moral views.

To see how this works, I will briefly examine
how three of Kohlberg's moral stages can influence
behavior in non-conflict situations. Consider a
stage 4 individual who eagerly enlists when his
country goes to war. No doubt there are many
factors involved in his desire to join. It
seems clear, though, that <u>one</u> factor is his moral
reasoning. He identifies right and wrong with
the interests of his country, and part of the
reason he wants to enlist is because he feels
he <u>should</u> enlist. This does not mean that every
stage 4 individual will eagerly enlist since, as
I mentioned, there are surely other motivational
factors. The point is that we can understand
the stage 4 person's action better by knowing the
kind of moral reasoning he employs. Similar
examples can be constructed for stage 3
individuals who rush into marriage, or stage 5
and 6 individuals who go into helping professions.
We can understand their vocational desires, in
part, by their moral beliefs.

The model of morality I am advocating, and
which I see as following from the cognitive
model of morality, is not merely a way to restrict behavior. Rather, it is an ordered set of
beliefs which guide our actions in many spheres.
One of Kohlberg's most interesting claims (which
to my knowledge he never explicitly states) is
that the degree to which we successfully restrict
our behavior vis-à-vis a moral principle or rule
is directly proportional to the usefulness of
that principle or rule in directing or suggesting
action in non-conflict situations. Of course,
conflict situations are those in which moral

beliefs are more easily detected. These instances, though, are cases where moral principles and beliefs become evident--this does not imply that their only function is to resolve these conflicts. Restricting certain kinds of behavior and resolving conflicts is undeniably an important part of morality; to concentrate on this aspect, however, leads to an inadequate conception of morality.

I have been trying to argue that the conception of morality on which cognitive moral psychology relies is superior to the official moral doctrines associated with psychoanalysis or social-learning theories. I argued as well that psychoanalysis, and therapy in general, must rely on this superior moral conception. This is because any therapy that attempts to give good reasons for or against moral beliefs is supposing that morality has a significant cognitive element. What I am attempting to show now is that the values that are discussed and tested in therapy are not restricted to the typical moral cases such as resolving conflicts or restricting behavior. These basic moral principles affect how a person directs many aspects of his life. Rogers presents a clear case of this. Since he attempts to lead the client to respect himself and others, and since this kind of belief can clearly form the basis of a moral system, we can view Rogerian therapy as a way to encourage a client to adopt definite and specific moral views. Rogers could reply that he is in no way attempting to alter the moral beliefs of the client; the point of therapy is to get the client to be more satisfied with himself, enabling him to live a happier life. What Rogers has discovered is that the person who respects himself in certain ways tends to be happier. Roger's reply would tend to support my view of moral beliefs and principles: I am suggesting that moral principles affect many spheres of our lives. What cognitive-developmental psychology has done is to present a way of understanding this by showing clear connections between moral and social development. Hence, a person who enters therapy because he "can't get along with others" is presenting a social problem, the solution of which will involve moral principles. All of this supports the view that the primary function of a person's morality is to direct his life both in conflict and non-conflict situations. Once again we can see that the strength of a principle in a conflict situation is related to how well the principle serves us in non-conflict situations.

This conception of morality and the function of morality requires a reevaluation of the arguments in 1.3.1. In that section I argued that moral issues could not be divorced from conceptions of mental health. The attitude I exhibited in those arguments was one of grudging acceptance: although it would be nice to elimi- nate moral issues from conceptions of mental health (it would eliminate a major therapeutic problem) this cannot be done. We can now begin to see why it would be undesirable to effect such a divorce. On the preferred conception of morality as a general action guide, it would be absurd to suggest that an activity (such as therapy) which attempts to help a person live better, could avoid influencing that person's moral principles.

The argument I have been presenting--that since moral principles affect many aspects of our lives, therapy is intimately concerned with them--does not seem too radical. A consequence of this argument, though, is that the healthy adult person is moral, and this may not only seem radical, but wrong. To see why it might not be so radical, and hence more acceptable, we need to make clear what this claim does not mean. First, it is not the claim that moral maturity is all that is needed to be mentally healthy; it simply asserts that moral maturity is a necessary condition for mental health in adults (Gilligan seems to hold this). Notice also that I am not saying that a specific form of morality is mature and hence necessary for mental health in adults. I am only making a statement about a connection between the concepts of "morality" and "mental health." Further, to say that the healthy adult must be moral is not to say anything about happiness. Clearly, a person could be both moral and healthy and still be terribly unhappy. Those who had the mental, moral, and physical stamina to survive brutal concentration camps, and generally those subject to great misfortune beyond their control, may be unhappy no matter how strong their mental and moral resources are.

3.3.1 A Brief Look at Some Connections Between Moral and Non-moral Issues in Therapy

The above discussion begins to indicate how moral and non-moral issues are related. If we take morality primarily as a way to decide what we will do, then it looks as though there will be non-moral ramifications of one's moral reasoning. Similarly, affecting the principles upon which a person's morality is founded in non-moral contexts can affect the person's moral thinking. In what follows, I will discuss four ways that moral and non-moral issues could influence one another in therapy.

A concrete connection between mental health and moral maturity is in terms of empathy and sympathy. It is relatively uncontroversial to assume that these sentiments are required for mental health. A rather severe disorder, sociopathy, is characterized by a lack of these sentiments. Beyond that, it is not controversial to suppose that a person who can coolly watch or participate in a wanton slaughter of another person is lacking normal human capacities. Kohlberg, as we saw earlier, argues that these two capacities are necessary for moral development. Without them, we cannot fully appreciate the nature of a moral conflict. Hence, both moral maturity and mental health require a sense of sympathy. Successful treatment of sociopathy, insofar as it results in an increase in sympathetic and empathetic responses, should have an effect on the morality of the individual.

Another connection between moral and non-moral issues was suggested in Chapter 1, when I pointed out that the way problems are solved in therapy may have an effect on a client's values. If we take therapy as involving a rational approach to problem solving, and we agree that morality admits rational considerations, then the application of this mode of problem solving to the moral realm may effect structural changes in the client's moral system. This could occur even if the client did not discuss moral problems in therapy. Szasz's theory is an example of this. He proposes that a therapist should not give answers to a client's particular questions (thus avoiding "moral" influence) but rather teach the client how to solve his own problems. What this means is that the client is being taught a way to solve problems. If the approach is one where reflection is important, digging out basic reasons and motives for behavior, it is clear how this activity might affect a person's moral structure if applied to moral problems.

A third connection can be discerned if we look to a common goal of therapy, viz., the improvement of a client's self-concept. We saw that Rogers explicitly mentioned this as a goal of therapy. The way to achieve this, for Rogers, is to let the client know that the therapist regards the client as important and worthy of respect. Rogers expresses this as an instance of the general principle that people have a certain worth and dignity. This principle is being imparted by Rogers to help the person attain a self-image that will allow him to feel better about himself; Rogers need not intend, as I mentioned above, to make the patient more

moral or to tamper with the client's moral
system. This is not to say, however, that the
principle imparted will not have a great effect
on the client's moral thinking. If he comes to
believe that persons are worthy of respect, and
begins to order his other beliefs in terms of
it, he will end up with a stage 5 or 6 conception
of morality. He will begin basing his moral
judgments, or explaining them, in these terms.
This is a case where a sound therapeutic non-
moral reason for altering a client's self-image
could drastically affect the client's moral
reasoning.

The final connection I want to discuss is
slightly different from the first three since it
rests on an empirical examination of the relationship between self-image and behavior associated
with the traditional virtue of benevolence. It
was found that persons who were generally happy
with themselves tended to exhibit more helping
behavior than those who were dissatisfied with
themselves.[178] Hence, if an improvement in self-
image tends to make one more satisfied with
oneself, there is reason to believe that this
shift promotes the traditional virtue of benevolence.

3.4   Indoctrination and Therapy

I tried to show in the beginning of Chapter 2
that the problem on which I am concentrating is
not the problem of indoctrination.[179] However,
indoctrination and the problem on which I am
working are similar: both are objectionable on
the ground that beliefs are acquired in uncritical
ways. Hence, this method of belief acquisition
is not one that distinguishes adequate from
inadequate beliefs. The real problem with a
client uncritically adopting beliefs or principles
found or exemplified in therapy is that, in
general, this is an unreliable method of belief
acquisition. The worry is not that the client

may become morally mature in therapy, or that he may become morally mature as a direct result of therapeutic influence. The problem is that some modes of moral belief acquisition are likely to maintain or prompt mental and moral immaturity. This worry, I think, was the basis of Mowrer's criticism of psychotherapy: the way analysts helped resolve moral problems seemed to lead the way to sociopathy or, at the very least, moral egoism. Mowrer's objection rests on viewing these as inadequate moral conceptions both for the individual and the group of which one is a member.

As we saw in Chapter 1, there are two basic ways that a therapist can affect the values of a client. He can alter the specific moral judgments that a client makes and the principles on the basis of which specific judgments are made. The way analysts and many therapists interpret morality is as a set of specific beliefs, acquired in a fairly direct manner from the social environment. Hence, to avoid moral influence they attempt to purge therapy of specific beliefs. This is the avowed method of the value-free thesis. Critics of this approach show, as I did, that it is impossible to eliminate specific moral values from therapy. Although this is true, such criticisms overlook the fact that there is more to moral development than acquiring particular values. This oversight prevents critics and proponents alike from seeing the real importance of the value-free thesis, viz., its emphasis on rationally examining moral beliefs. It is the emphasis on critically reviewing moral beliefs and attitudes which makes the value-free thesis tenable. Once we see that a person's morality has different aspects which can be affected in different ways, the problem of a client uncritically adopting values in therapy must be recast.

On the analysis of the problem I am presenting, the presence of moral principles in concepts

of mental health and the fact that a therapist
cannot hide his moral convictions is not in
itself relevant. The question is, can a
therapist direct therapy in a way that minimizes
the chance of these being uncritically adopted?
That is, can we understand therapy as a place
where values can be discussed without viewing
that as presenting material which will be
arbitrarily adopted by the client?

I think the cognitive conception of morality
gives us a way to see how and why this is
possible. Cognitive moral development views a
person's moral system as one that develops in
order to cope with problems. Since one's
morality serves to direct one's behavior, a
major problem arises when that moral scheme is
unable to suggest how one should act. This can
arise for two reasons: 1) two beliefs suggest
incompatible actions, or 2) there is no belief or
principle that applies to the problem. In
either case we can see that moral change is
related to a specific problem, and that the
change will be specific as well. In the first
kind of problem some belief will have to be
taken as prior to another, and in the second
case a new principle must be figured out, or at
least a new understanding of some principle
already held will be required. These specific
changes, though, can infect our entire moral
system. On our analysis, one undergoes structural
moral change only when one's moral system is
perceived as inadequate in some way. Significant
moral change of this variety will not occur
simply because a therapist emphasizes this or
that belief. The studies on passive exposure of
varying moral beliefs show that there is no
significant incidence of these beliefs being
acquired.[180]

A cognitive theory of moral development also
shows why a value-free approach need not have
the consequences Mowrer predicted. Mowrer's fear
was that a value-free approach would de-emphasize

moral issues, thus leading a client to reject
moral limitations as binding. On our view,
however, delving into the reasons behind moral
views and questioning their validity need not
weaken morality and can often strengthen it.
That is, although this type of process is the
one that is most likely to reveal inadequacies
in one's moral views, the "natural" reaction to
finding these problems is not to reject morality
altogether but rather to construct a new moral
system, using the old one as a base, that overcomes these problems. This would explain
Gilligan's observation that his method of getting
a client to reject morality (in terms of guilt)
does not result in unbridled egoism or sociopathy. Gilligan's method is not aimed at
rejecting morality, but at rejecting inadequate
moral systems.

Also, a cognitive theory of value development preserves the way most therapists conceive
of their own activity. As we saw in Chapter 1,
Hartmann, Szasz and Rogers all described uncritical value adoption on the part of a client as
antithetical to the goal of therapy. Although
these therapists may disagree about what constitutes effective therapy, they all concurred
that a client should not blindly believe in the
values expressed in therapy.

How does our cognitive program of emphasizing
reasoning measure up to the requirements of
personal autonomy with which Hartmann, Szasz
and Rogers were concerned? An obstacle to
answering this is the difficulty of formulating
a notion of moral autonomy. Although we have
clear intuitions that people should be free to
choose their own spouses, careers, schools and
religions, is it equally clear that we are free
to develop our own moral codes? If a person
feels that the proper penalty for theft is
death or that people who do not live by a
specific code are evil, is he free to act on
those beliefs? Although there may be great

latitude in the moral beliefs from which one can act, this does not mean there are no limits whatsoever.

Despite the problem of where to draw the line with respect to moral autonomy, the emphasis on reasoning will, I think, avoid the charge of violating personal autonomy. Violating such autonomy must at least have the feature of forcing or tricking another to adopt moral values. On our view of moral development, the program of emphasizing reasons does everything possible to insure that the basic moral values which a client adopts in therapy will be evaluated critically.

We can now reevaluate the two modes of influence in therapy discussed in Chapter 1, viz., therapeutic and therapist influence. It seems that the moral views found in theories of therapy would induce a client to restructure his moral system. This, as we have seen, is unobjectionable as long as the therapist concentrates on the reasons that this is a good way to organize moral beliefs, or a good way to approach problems. The door is left open for the client to go on to examine these reasons. Rogers does not attempt to pound in the principle of respecting oneself or others, but attempts to get the client to see the reasonableness of this view. Doing this requires a delicate technique; but I think it is best analyzed as the process of making the client aware of his own beliefs, motives, habits, thus allowing the client to use his own reasoning to sort out his problems. This, I judge, is perfectly legitimate.

Therapist influence, however, presents a slightly different problem. Insofar as a person's moral attitudes and beliefs are transmitted, often on an unconscious level, it looks as though uncritical adoption of the therapist's moral beliefs is not something that can be avoided. This, however, looks bad only if we view it in isolation from therapeutic influence. If a therapist is successful in helping a client examine the reasons for his beliefs and getting the client to examine the point of those beliefs, uncritical adoption of the therapist's moral beliefs should be relatively insignificant. A client who has gained the ability to search out his motives and examine these is equally capable of subjecting the beliefs he acquires in this way to the same kind of criticism; in fact it is conceivable that this should be discussed in therapy. Of course, there is still the problem that a client might not be psychologically capable of evaluating what the therapist says. In such a case presenting reasons may not effectively guard against the client uncritically adopting moral beliefs. This does not bear on our problem though: the responsibility of the therapist is to do all he can to prevent uncritical adoption of moral beliefs. If a therapist gives <u>reasons</u> for his views, he is at least setting up the framework for examining the values being expressed in therapy. In this case, the therapist is doing all he can to prevent a client from non-rationally adopting beliefs as well as giving the client a way of evaluating beliefs that may be adopted in therapy in a non-rational way. This is not indoctrination, nor is it avoiding the moral issues.

But what if there are significant non-rational forces important in moral development, as we discussed in 3.2.1. Could therapy unwittingly affect these aspects of a person's morality? As we suggested earlier, it is likely that "non-rational" factors of moral development, such as habits, are not entirely non-rational, but have significant cognitive components. But even if there are determinants of moral behavior that are non-rational, and it could be shown that therapy has an effect on these, our solution is still viable. By concentrating on the justification of these non-rational modes of behavior, a client could come to either accept the behavior or reject it. Of course, to eliminate non-rationally motivated behavior would require that the person have a knowledge of the mechanisms which underlie that behavior. Drug taking by a drug addict is a good example of this. Since there is a physical need to acquire the drug, this can be interpreted as non-rationally motivated behavior. Although a person may deplore the habit for moral reasons, it is clear that the decision to stop taking the drugs will require more than the simple judgment that drug addiction is morally wrong. Once one has decided to stop, further measures must be taken such as removing oneself from the availability of drugs, and insuring medical treatment during withdrawal. These are reasonable ways to deal with a habit which is partly rooted in physiological dependence. This is an extreme example, but it shows that if non-rational modes of behavior are developed in therapy, then these can be subjected to the same critical review to which values are subjected. Once again, a goal of therapy is to give the client the ability to evaluate values critically, whether or not they are acquired in therapy.

One last objection to my approach is the following: the reason-belief distinction on which I rely may be thought to be untenable. To offer a reason, it may be said, is to offer a belief. Ultimately, therefore, there is no way to avoid belief imposition; to emphasize reasons is to emphasize beliefs. The reply to this is to clarify the approach I am recommending. I am not suggesting that a therapist offer a set of reasons as the ultimate justification of select beliefs. Rather, the therapist should emphasize the reasoning process, the relation between reasons and beliefs. Admittedly, the only way this can be done is by offering, or encouraging the client to offer, specific reasons for specific beliefs. On the cognitive view of moral learning we can see why this need not result in an uncritical adoption of reasons a therapist might suggest.

The solution to the problem of a client uncritically adopting values in therapy is based on the rational nature of moral development. This does not mean that moral commands can be formulated using reason alone. It simply means that the values to which we are exposed, and which we may be pressured to adopt, can be evaluated using rational criteria. We have also seen that the basic criteria which people employ are the criteria we use to evaluate all theories, namely, consistency and explanatory power. Therapists can avoid being doctrinaire and encouraging uncritical adoption of moral values in therapy even though such values cannot be eliminated. This does not imply that this is an easy task, or one that will always be successful. What it does show is that uncritical value adoption in therapy can be dealt with in a salutary way.

[137]It may be that this kind of example could be used to _justify_ indoctrination in certain cases. If the advisee is so disturbed that he cannot understand the reasons, emphasis on reasons may have to be neglected.

[138]Ibid., p. 44.

[139]Ibid., p. 55.

[140]Ibid., p. 46.

[141]Ibid., p. 51.

[142]Ibid., p. 64.

[143]Richard McKeon, ed., _The Basic Works of Aristotle_, pp. 950-951.

[144]Ibid., p. 952.

[145]Ibid., p. 953.

[146]James Wallace, "Excellences and Merit," pp. 192-195.

[147]James Wallace, _Virtues and Vices_, pp. 78, 81.

[148]For more on this and related problems, see William P. Alston, "Traits, Consistency and Conceptual Alternatives for Personality Theory," p. 20 ff.

[149]Hugh Hartshorne and Mark May, _Studies in the Organization of Character_, p. 1.

[150]Hartshorne and May, _Studies in Service and Self-Control_, p. 453.

[151] Hartshorne and May, Studies in the Organization of Character, p. 377.

[152] Ibid., p. 373.

[153] Kohlberg, "Stages of Moral Development," p. 75.

[154] Ibid., p. 79.

[155] Ibid., p. 78.

[156] Ibid.

[157] John Dewey, Human Nature and Conduct, p. 40.

[158] Kohlberg, "Stages of Moral Development," p. 55.

[159] Melvin Funk, Moral Judgments and Neuroses, p. 4.

[160] James Gilligan, "Beyond Morality."

[161] Ibid., p. 144.

[162] Ibid., p. 145.

[163] Ibid.

[164] Ibid., p. 144.

[165] Ibid.

[166] Ibid.

[167] Ibid., p. 150.

[168] Ibid., p. 145.

[169] Ibid., p. 156.

[170] Ibid.

[171] Ibid., p. 158.

[172] Ibid.

[173] I say that judgment is "conceptually prior" to the feeling since it is unlikely that it is temporally prior. That is, it seems likely that the judgment (reflective or unreflective) and the feeling "occur" together.

[174] Gilligan, p. 145.

[175] For more on this see William P. Alston, "Moral Attitudes and Moral Judgments."

[176] Gilligan, p. 153.

[177] See Freud, Civilization and Its Discontents.

[178] Martin Hoffman, "Developmental Synthesis of Affect and Cognition and its Implications for Altruistic Motivation," p. 608.

[179] This is not to say that indoctrination should not be avoided, it is just that it is not the problem with which I am concerned.

[180] Kohlberg, "From Is To Ought," p. 194.

BIBLIOGRAPHY

Alston, William P. "Comments on Kohlberg's
    'From Is To Ought.'" In Cognitive Develop-
    ment and Epistemology, edited by Theodore
    Mischel. New York: Academic Press, 1971.

_____. "Moral Attitudes and Moral Judgments."
    Nous, vol. 2, no. 1, 1968.

_____. "Toward a Logical Geography of
    Personality: Traits and Deeper Lying
    Personality Characteristics." In Mind,
    Science and History, vol. 2. Albany:
    University of New York Press, 1970.

_____. "Traits, Consistency and Conceptual
    Alternatives for Personality Theory."
    Journal for the Theory of Social Behavior,
    vol. 5, no. 1, 1975.

Aristotle. The Basic Works of Aristotle, edited
    by Richard McKeon. New York: Random House,
    1968.

Bell, Norman W., and Vogel, Ezra F. A Modern
    Introduction to the Family. New York: The
    Free Press, 1960.

Blatt, N., and Kohlberg, L. "Effects of Class-
    room Discussion on Moral Thought." In
    Recent Research in Moral Development, edited
    by Lawrence Kohlberg and Elliot Turiel.
    New York: Holt, Rinehart and Winston, 1971.

Buhler, Charlotte. Values in Psychotherapy.
    New York: The Free Press of Glencoe, 1962.

Campagna, Anthony F., and Harter, Susan. "Moral
    Judgment in Sociopathic and Normal Children."
    Journal of Personality and Social Psychology,
    vol. 31, no. 2, 1975.

Chandler, Hugh. "Hedonism." American Philosophi-
     cal Quarterly, vol. 12, no. 3, 1975.

Dewey, John. Human Nature and Conduct. New York:
     The Modern Library, 1957.

Diggs, B. J. The State, Justice and the Common
     Good. Glenview: Scott, Foresman and Co.,
     1974.

Donegan, Alan. "Mr. Hare and the Conscientious
     Nazi." Philosophical Studies, vol. 16,
     no. 1-2, 1965.

Duska, Richard, and Whelan, M. Moral Development:
     A Guide to Piaget and Kohlberg. New York:
     Paulist Press, 1975.

Epicurus. "Principal Doctrines." In Approaches
     to Ethics, edited by W. T. Jones, Frederick
     Sontag, et al. New York: McGraw Hill Book
     Co., 1977.

Frankena, William K. Ethics. Englewood Cliffs:
     Prentice Hall, Inc., 1973.

_____. "Value and Valuation." In The
     Encyclopedia of Philosophy, vol. 8, edited
     by Paul Edwards. New York: Macmillan
     Publishing Co., Inc., 1967.

Freud, Sigmund. "Civilization and Its Discon-
     tents." In The Complete Psychological Works
     of Sigmund Freud, vol. 2, edited and
     translated by James Strachey. London:
     Hogarth Press, 1961.

_____. The Ego and the Id, translated by
     Joan Riviere. The International Psycho-
     Analytical Library, no. 12, edited by
     Ernest Jones. London: Hogarth Press, 1927.

_____. "On Narcissism: An Introduction."
In The Complete Psychological Works of
Sigmund Freud, vol. 14, edited and trans-
lated by James Strachey. London: Hogarth
Press, 1957.

Friedman, Max W. Discussant in "Values and their
Relationship to Psychiatric Principles and
Practice," by S. W. Ginsburg and J. L. Herma.
American Journal of Psychotherapy, vol. 7,
no. 3, 1953.

Funk, Melvin. Moral Judgment and Neurosis. Ph.D.
Dissertation, University of Illinois, 1961.

Gilligan, James. "Beyond Morality." In Moral
Development and Behavior, edited by T.
Lickona. New York: Holt, Rinehart and
Winston, 1976.

Goldstein, Kurt. "Health as a Value." In New
Knowledge in Human Values, edited by Abraham
Maslow. New York: Harper and Brothers,
1959.

Hampshire, Stuart. Two Theories of Morality.
Oxford: Oxford University Press, 1977.

Hare, R. M. Freedom and Reason. London: Oxford
University Press, 1965.

Hartmann, Heinz. Psychoanalysis and Moral Values.
New York: International Press, Inc., 1960.

Hartshorne, Hugh, and May, Mark. Studies in
Deceit. Studies in the Nature of Character,
vol. I. New York: The Macmillan Co., 1928.

_____. Studies in Service and Self-Control.
Studies in the Nature of Character, vol. II.
New York: The Macmillan Co., 1929.

_____. Studies in the Organization of Character. Studies in the Nature of Character, vol. III. New York: The Macmillan Co., 1930.

Hoffman, Martin. "Developmental Synthesis of Affect and Cognition and Its Implications for Altruistic Motivation." Developmental Psychology, vol. 11, no. 5, 1975.

Hook, Sydney, ed. Psychoanalysis, Scientific Method and Philosophy. New York: New York University Press, 1959.

Kant, Immanuel. Groundwork of the Metaphysic of Morals, translated by H. J. Paton. New York: Harper Torchbooks, 1964.

Kellman, Harold, and Diethelm, Oskar. "Goals in Therapy: A Round Table Discussion." The American Journal of Psychoanalysis, vol. 16, no. 1, 1956.

Kohlberg, Lawrence. "From Is to Ought." In Cognitive Development and Epistemology, edited by Theodore Mischel. New York: Academic Press, 1971.

_____. "Moral Development and Identification." In Child Psychology, 62nd Yearbook of the National Society for the Study of Education, edited by H. Stevenson. Chicago: University of Chicago Press, 1963.

_____. "Stages of Moral Development as a Basis for Moral Education." In Moral Education: Interdisciplinary Approaches, edited by C. M. Beck, B. S. Crittenden and E. Sullivan. Toronto: University of Toronto Press, 1971.

Kohlberg, Lawrence, and Turiel, Elliot. "Moral Development and Moral Education." In Psychology and Educational Practice, edited by G. S. Lessor. Glenview: Scott Foresman and Co., 1971.

Locke, Don. "The Trivializability of Universalizability." Philosophical Review, vol. 77, no. 1, 1968.

Margolis, Joseph. Psychotherapy and Morality. New York: Random House, 1966.

Mischel, Walter, and Mischel, Harriet N. "A Cognitive Social-Learning Approach to Morality and Self-Regulation." In Moral Development and Behavior, edited by T. Lickona. New York: Holt, Rinehart and Winston, 1976.

Mowrer, O. H. "New Evidence Concerning the Nature of Psychopathology." Buffalo Studies, vol. 4, no. 2, 1968.

Mowrer, O. H., and Vattano, Anthony J. Integrity Groups. Urbana, Il.: Integrity Groups, 1975.

Murphy, Arthur E. The Theory of Practical Reason, edited by A. E. Melden. La Salle: Open Court, 1955.

Patterson, C. H. Counseling and Psychotherapy: Theory and Practice. New York: Harper and Row, Publishers, 1959.

Pepper, Stephen C. The Sources of Value. Berkeley: University of California Press, 1958.

Piers, Gerhart, and Singer, Milton. Shame and Guilt. New York: W. W. Norton and Co., 1971.

Rawls, John. "Justification of Civil Disobedience." In Civil Disobedience: Theory and Practice, edited by H. A. Bedau. Indianapolis: Pegusus, 1969.

_____. A Theory of Justice. Cambridge: The Belknap Press of Harvard University Press, 1971.

Rogers, Carl R. Client-Centered Therapy. Boston: Houghton Mifflin Co., 1965.

_____. On Becoming a Person. London: Constable and Co., Ltd., 1967.

Sears, Robert; Rau, Lucy; Alpert, Richard. Identification and Child Rearing. Stanford: Stanford University Press, 1965.

Smart, J. C. C. Utilitarianism For and Against. Cambridge: University Press, 1973.

Snook, I. A. Indoctrination and Education. London: Routledge and Keagan Paul, 1972.

Standal, S. W., and Corsini, R. J. Critical Incidents in Psychotherapy. New Jersey: Prentice Hall, Inc., 1959.

Sterba, Richard. "The Formative Activity of the Analyst." International Journal of Psycho-analysis, vol. 25, no. 1-2, 1944.

Szasz, Thomas. The Ethics of Psychoanalysis. New York: Basic Books, Inc., 1965.

Turiel, Elliot. "Conflict and Transition in Adolescent Moral Development." Child Development, vol. 45, no. 1, 1974.

Wallace, James. "Excellences and Merit." Philosophical Review, vol. 83, no. 2, 1974.

_____. "Practical Inquiry." Philosophical Review, vol. 78, no. 4, 1969.

_____. Virtues and Vices. Ithica: Cornell University Press, 1978.

Wilder, Joseph. Discussant in "Values and Their
Relationship to Psychiatric Principles and
Practice," by S. W. Ginsburg and J. L. Herma.
American Journal of Psychotherapy, vol. 7,
no. 3, 1953.

Wisdom, John. Philosophy and Psychoanalysis.
New York: Philosophical Library, 1953.

Wolberg, Lewis R. The Technique of Psychotherapy.
New York, 1954.

Wrightsman, Lawrence. Social Psychology.
Monteray: Brooks/Cole Publishing Co., 1972.

Wrightsman, Lawrence, and Brigam, John C.
Contemporary Issues in Social Psychology.
Monteray: Brooks/Cole Publishing Co.,
1973.

Yalom, Irving. The Theory and Practice of Group
Psychotherapy. New York: Basic Books,
1975.

John William Dienhart was born in Evanston, Illinois on December 13, 1949. He graduated from Evanston Township High School in 1967. He received his B.A. from Roosevelt University, which he attended from 1967 to 1972. Following his graduation from Roosevelt, he accepted a Graduate Assistantship at the University of Illinois at Urbana which he held until 1977. He received his Ph.D. from the University of Illinois in August, 1979. He has held teaching positions at the University of Illinois, Illinois Wesleyan University and Illinois State University. He is presently teaching at St. Cloud State University.